Allan Morrison is the author of 14 books with sales well in advance of a quarter of a million copies. Media appearances include *Richard and Judy*, *The One Show* and the *Fred McAulay Show*. Allan is a Rotarian and a very popular after-dinner speaker. Now retired, he enjoys raising funds for local charities, bagging Munros and lives in the west of Scotland with his wife.

Let's Get Married

The Lighter Side of Love, Romance and Weddings

Allan Morrison

hachette
SCOTLAND

First published in 2010 by
HACHETTE SCOTLAND, an imprint of
HACHETTE UK

1

Cataloguing in Publication Data is available from the British Library

ISBN 978 0 7553 1950 3

Illustrations © Rupert Besley

Designed and typeset by Susie Bell

Printed and bound in Great Britain by Clays Ltd, St Ives plc

Hachette Scotland's policy is to use papers that are natural, renewable and recyclable products and made from wood grown in sustainable forests. The logging and manufacturing processes are expected to conform to the environmental regulations of the country of origin.

HACHETTE SCOTLAND
An Hachette UK Company
338 Euston Road
London NW1 3BH

www.hachettescotland.co.uk
www.hachette.co.uk

My grateful thanks goes to Craig Morrison, Lynne Roper, Anne McGregor and Val Stevenson for their assistance with this book.

Contents

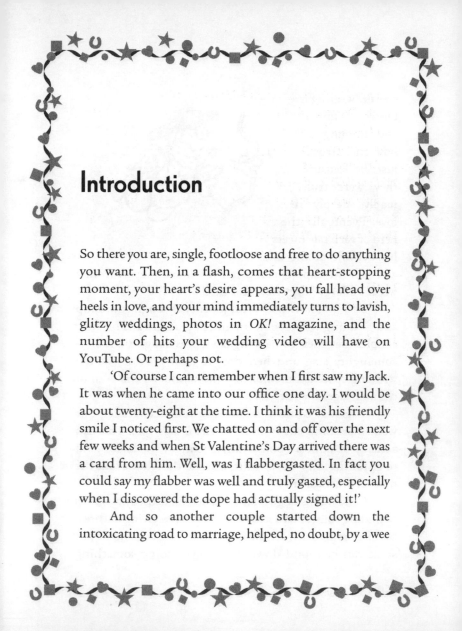

Introduction

So there you are, single, footloose and free to do anything you want. Then, in a flash, comes that heart-stopping moment, your heart's desire appears, you fall head over heels in love, and your mind immediately turns to lavish, glitzy weddings, photos in *OK!* magazine, and the number of hits your wedding video will have on YouTube. Or perhaps not.

'Of course I can remember when I first saw my Jack. It was when he came into our office one day. I would be about twenty-eight at the time. I think it was his friendly smile I noticed first. We chatted on and off over the next few weeks and when St Valentine's Day arrived there was a card from him. Well, was I flabbergasted. In fact you could say my flabber was well and truly gasted, especially when I discovered the dope had actually signed it!'

And so another couple started down the intoxicating road to marriage, helped, no doubt, by a wee cherub wearing a tartan bunnet and holding a bow and arrow, just to ensure they were truly, madly, deeply in love. Eventually the hero of each tale meets his heroine at the altar and they live happily ever after. Well mostly, apart from a wee bit of argy-bargy now and then.

Let's Get Married is a fun journey through courtship and weddings. The book includes actual details on how couples met, their romancing days, plus naughty and not-so-naughty stag and hen dos. It then provides actual wedding speeches, memories of honeymoons and even of the marriages themselves.

This may come as a shock to you, dear reader, but women are different from men. *Vive la différence!* This can actually be quite a good arrangement, for the ladies tend to go for the lovey-dovey stuff, whereas the fellows take the macho, practical angle.

Generations of girls have mastered the tricky business of finding someone to marry, perhaps even giving nature a bit of a hand to attract the boys. As for the lads, no doubt some can be found down at the gym doing something

 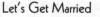

about their pecs, or in the local topping up on Dutch courage before going out on the pull.

Unfortunately it has to be said some Scottish men are utterly selfish. They call themselves bachelors; a man who never makes the same mistake once. But if they do opt to marry, at what age should they do so? Well, actually there are three ages of Scotsmen. Under age, over age and average.

Choosing a husband is like choosing a kitchen: you ignore the way it is and picture how it's going to be once you've remodelled it. So, when the courtship has finished, and the girl has decided who has made the cut and she can't do any better for a soul mate (despite going online for a final trawl through *Bachelor of the Month* dating sites), then the next stage is the time-honoured ritual of a wedding. Most women just love weddings, for a woman's heart resembles the moon: there's always a man in it. And anyway weddings are the *real* climax of the outpouring of passion and love.

And what is this thing called love? Love should never be stymied, because love is the feeling that you overwhelmingly feel when you feel you're going to feel a feeling that you've never felt before. (Know what I mean?)

Many consider Scotland as the *top* romantic wedding country. Venues abound in this magical land, ranging from the world-famous Gretna Green, where wedding ceremonies have taken place over the anvil since 1754, to romantic settings at one of our many castles. Imagine dancing in breathtaking splendour with crystal chandeliers above your head as you twirl the night away.

We do indeed have a beautiful country in which to celebrate our wedding traditions. Many second-, third- and even fourth-generation Scots arrive from overseas for their marriage ceremony as they wish to be at home with their roots, hear the skirl of the bagpipes, and be proud of the distinctive look of our national dress. A-list celebrities from all over the world also come to Scotland to 'plight their troth' including Ashley Judd, Stella McCartney, Jennifer Ehle, Madonna and J. K. Rowling. And not forgetting members of the royal family such as Princess Anne.

Yes, times have changed, and with it plenty of variations on the theme of love, ranging from civil partnerships for same-sex couples, to Apache wedding blessings. Declarations of love have also changed from sweet billets-doux to constant streams of texts.

Some Scots opt to have their weddings abroad, perhaps exchanging their vows on a sun-kissed beach in the Caribbean, or having a *Mamma Mia!* marriage on a Greek Island; maybe in the wedding chapels of Las Vegas, or indeed over the sea in Skye, Rothesay or Arran. Then back to Scotland, or in the case of the Scottish Isles back to the mainland, for the big hoolie with family and friends.

Love is big business because it makes the world go round. Just think on some of the many films which feature weddings: *Father of the Bride*; *Muriel's Wedding*; *Guess Who's*

Coming to Dinner; I Love You, Man; My Big Fat Greek Wedding; The Wedding Planner; Monsoon Wedding; Runaway Bride; My Best Friend's Wedding; Bride Wars; Pride (and, for that matter, *Bride*) *and Prejudice.*

Anticipation of the great event can almost generate as much excitement as the wedding itself. After months, perhaps years, the great day arrives, but not without the rituals of the stag and hen nights. Nowadays, with the

advent of cheap flights, it could be a knees-up in New York, Prague or Paris, as against a few drinks in the local. Then it's on with the big show and it could be a very big show indeed. Perhaps dinner for up to two hundred people or the couple may just opt for carry-oots with fried Mars bars for dessert all washed down with Irn-Bru.

A good Scottish marriage is a precious thing. The question is, are you prepared to face this person over countless breakfasts of porridge or Kellogg's Special K? Real love is a combination of qualities: admiration, affection, co-operation, honour, sacrifice and respect. Marriage is not merely a lifestyle choice, it also involves falling in love many times, but always with the same person, for that one individual can touch your heart like no other.

But you must always remember one important fact: marriage does change everything... suddenly you will find yourself in bed with a relative.

Please note that many of the names of people in this book have been changed to protect the innocent... and the 'not-so-innocent'!

Chapter One: 'Hallowrerr!'

The Thrill of the Chase

A man usually feels better after a few winks, especially if she winks back

Where did you meet the one you love? At the pub or club? At work, school or university? Maybe surfing the net, speed dating, personal columns, or via a dating agency? Perhaps you nursed a passion for the wee lad or lassie next door? Or did your eyes first meet across a crowded wedding reception?

In Scotland there is very little change in the weather throughout the year, which is probably the reason young

Scots' fancy turns to thoughts of love in spring, summer, autumn and even winter, too. In other words they are continually eyeing up the talent. The problem with this is that the Scottish girl or guy may get through an awful lot of 'testers' before they make their final selection.

But take great care. They must be chosen carefully. It's like selecting fruit. They must be fresh but not too young. They must be tender and ripe for the picking. Just watch they're not past their sell-by date.

Experts studying what makes for a long-lasting and loving relationship observe that couples still in love well past the seven-year itch tend to recall fondly, regularly and indeed vividly their first meeting. It has not been unknown for couples to exchange cards on what they call their 'meet-anniversary' and their first 'snog-anniversary'.

An informal survey of some modern Scottish women yielded the following. Women want a man who will: show them respect; open doors for them (maybe into the bedroom); pay their way; be honest with them (except when asked, 'Does my bum look big in this?'); hold their hand; make them laugh; and in whom they can have confidence.

And as for men, researchers have found that all they want is a younger version of their mother, and a bit of encouragement.

Farmer Donald and Heather were walking along a Highland country path in the late evening. Heather said,

'Donald, I am afraid.' Asked Donald, 'Och, and what wid ye be afraid of?' Said Heather, 'I'm afraid you might give me a wee kiss.' Answered Donald, 'And how could I kiss you with me carrying two buckets and with a hen under each arm?' Said Heather, 'I was afraid you might put a hen under each bucket and then kiss me.'

Another factor is looks. They say that as God made them he matched them. Yes, for many people love is blind, but at least it seems to be able to find its way around in the dark. Love is the key element for marrying the perfect partner. Merely marrying for looks is like buying a house for its paint. You must ask, 'Is he a Don Juan or the man our children will look up to?'

Remember that if you have elderly relatives who come up to you at weddings and dig you in the ribs and say, 'You're next' then the only way to stop this sort of nonsense is to do the same to them at funerals... or get married.

How did some Scots Find their Perfect Mr and Mrs Right?

Georgina's Story

'I went to a speed dating session at an Edinburgh hotel. There were different categories in various rooms. One was for "The Young", women aged 23-45 and men 25-47. Another was a "Toy Boy Special" for women aged 43–59 and men 23–39. Or you could go for the "Sugar Daddy Special" for women 23–39 and men 45–whatever. Needless to say I went for "The Young" session.

Are you Fit Attractive Male (39) with GSOH waiting to meet Slim Brunette, keen on fast cars and smart restaurants?

'Before sitting down at the first table I had a quick look round the room and number fourteen immediately took my eye. As I looked at him he looked at me. When I got to his table we both knew, as we confessed to each other later, that that was it. By the time the bell went I had ticked all his boxes and he had ticked mine. I thought to myself, "If I could just kiss him once I'd die happy." Now we've been together for three years. I just love him. Good old speed dating, I say.'

♥ YOU CAN'T KISS A SCOTTISH LASS UNEXPECTEDLY. YOU CAN ONLY KISS HER SOONER THAN SHE THOUGHT YOU WOULD.

Julie's Story

'Believe it or not I met him through the internet. He was someone with a GSOH [good sense of humour], who was looking for love with someone who would BFF [be friends forever] – so far so good – and would not be against PDA [public displays of affection], now limited, I must admit, to an occasional wee cheeper in the street.

'First of all we met for a little dinner à deux, and the next day there was a bunch of red roses delivered to my flat. He was and is charm personified. A week later I got a love letter plus a poem he had specially composed. Well, that was me in a tizzy of love, sure it was. Three months later we were carving our initials on a tree in the park. Not very eco-friendly but oh, so romantic.'

'LOOK AT THAT LASS WALKIN' ALANG THE PROMENADE.'
'WHIT'S SHE DOING?'
'SHE'S LOOKING FOR HER MAN.'
'OH, WHIT'S HIS NAME?'
'SHE DOESNAE KNOW YET.'

Davina's Story

'I've been out with stacks of guys I found on dating sites. It used to be exciting but having met a few beauties who turned out to be nothing like their photo or description, I got a bit disheartened. Then I went to a party with a Bonnie Scotland theme, and there was "the one", Paul. I actually found the man of my dreams. I am so, so, lucky. He is loving, considerate, and makes me laugh. I am still in the first throes of passion. Story book stuff, really. Lucky old me.'

A MODEST GIRL NEVER PURSUES A MAN, NOR DOES A MOUSETRAP PURSUE A MOUSE.

Bruce's Story

'It was a blind date arranged by my friend Wallace. He eventually was my best man. It was in this hotel in George Street. She was late but when she came into the bar area I knew that it was my date.

'She sort of glided across the room in this black dress. Wow! She looked just perfect. It turned out that she was a bit of the independent type and she was honest enough to tell me she had been round the block a few times. Mind you I had been round more than a few blocks myself.

'She said she was romantic and at thirty-one was still looking for love. She thought that a couple of her previous men might have married her but she didn't quite feel the same. She said she wasn't "truly, madly, deeply", in love with them.

'She turned out to be very frank and honest about her romantic liaisons, even talked about her hormones, not something I am an expert in. Anyway we got on like a house on fire and had a great old chinwag for hours.

'In the months after our initial meeting our romance blossomed and it just seemed logical we should eventually marry. I don't actually remember proposing as such, it just was kind of assumed by both of us.'

♥ 'IF YOU ARE EVER IN DOUBT AS TO WHETHER OR NOT YOU SHOULD KISS A PRETTY GIRL, ALWAYS GIVE HER THE BENEFIT OF THE DOUBT.

Andrew's Story

'You no doubt remember the old Scottish song "Jeannie McCall, Ah met her at a waddin' in the Co-operative hall". Well, I met Liz in the queue at the local Co-op. She was paying her bill in cash and was a pound short, so as I had been standing behind her, admiring her nice figure if you really want the truth, I immediately offered her a pound coin. She refused, took back the cash she had already handed to the assistant, and paid by credit card.

'Outside the shop she was putting her shopping bags in the boot of her car, but stopped to smile and say "Thank you" for my offer. It turned out she lived almost sixty miles away but was doing some shopping for an old aunt. After a bit of chat I could tell she sort of liked me so I asked her for a date. During our time courting my car put on over twenty thousand miles. Eventually I stayed overnight and then I would find little love letters in my brief case at work the following day.'

♥ 'WHEN YOU MEET SOMEONE WHO CAN COOK AND DO HOUSEWORK, DON'T HESITATE... MARRY HIM.

Susan's Story

'We met on an internet dating site. His photo was not exactly inspiring but our interests were very similar. We met and it took off from there. You could say we just "Double Clicked"!'

♥ .'WOMEN ARE LIKE MOBILE PHONES. THEY LOVE TO BE HELD, LOVE TO BE TALKED TO, BUT IF YOU PRESS THE WRONG BUTTON... YOU GET DISCONNECTED.

Peter's Story

'I was at a party with another girl. In fact the party was being given by her sister. I was chatting away to someone when I saw this big smile across the room. It was a kind of goofy, almost bashful, smile. It wasn't directed at me but I couldn't help but be attracted to her. Eventually I managed to get her attention. I think I had fallen for her by then. I asked for her mobile number but she couldn't remember it. So I gave her mine. I thought she wouldn't phone but thankfully she did. What a lovely warm person she is; and what a great kisser! Every moment is precious and pertinent. We are now to be married next year.'

♥ 'IF LOVE IS BLIND, WHY IS LINGERIE SO POPULAR?

Samantha's Story

'I eventually became a "mistletoe bride". It was at a Christmas party we first met. Initially I didn't really fancy him in the least. However, one of his mates held mistletoe over us, we kissed and that was the start of things. In fact, during his wedding speech James referred to this and then produced a sprig of mistletoe and kissed me. Everybody clapped and cheered.'

♥ 'LOVE IS A CARD GAME. GET RID OF THE JOKERS, FIND AN ACE IN DIAMONDS, OR TRY TO GET A KING.

Mary's Story

'I first saw Bill at the tennis club. I think it was his cheeky grin that caught my attention. Eventually he partnered me at doubles and we went on to win the club championship, by which time he was seeing me home with mushy kisses in the car outside my house. I am sure to this day my mother was behind the curtains having a quick squint. Eventually I invited him home for a meal. Later my father actually said that I could do worse than settle for Bill. It turned out to be good advice.'

♥ TWO WEE BOYS WERE PLAYING WHEN A CUTE, BLONDE GIRL WALKED BY. 'SEE WHEN I STOP HATING GIRLS,' SAID ONE OF THE LADS, 'I THINK I'LL STOP HATING THAT ONE FIRST.'

Rita's Story

'I used dating and matching sites for about four months. I was lucky and met some nice guys. I always emailed them and spoke to them by phone before we met up. And I always made sure it was in a public place. Actually there is quite a thrill in anticipating meeting up with someone who could be the right one for you.

'The first time I arranged to meet someone I had my sister watching from across the road. The dates were all fun; though for many of them, the photos they had put on the website must have been taken years ago!

'Then I met David. It certainly wasn't love at first sight but I sort of felt comfortable with him. Even my fussy sister quite likes him. Now we are going to get married, so there is no longer any need for any more dating sites.'

♥ LOVE IS A GAME.
YET BOTH CAN PLAY
AND BOTH CAN WIN.

Lorna's Story

'It was our second date and we were sitting in Pizza Express. We both stopped eating at the same time, looked at each other, and I believe that was the moment. The all-consuming heart-racing romance had started. Talk about the moon hitting your eye like a big pizza pie! Good job I was sitting down or I would have been swept off my feet.'

♥ SOMETIMES YOU HAVE TO KISS A FEW FROGS BEFORE
YOU FIND YOUR PRINCE.

James's Story

'We met through a dating agency. She wanted someone who liked people, wasn't tall, liked more formal attire and whose sport was swimming. I told her she would have been better off with a penguin.

'After we were married she told me that her mother had said that I wasn't much to look at, but at least thought I was nice, and anyway I would be at work most of the time.'

'MY GIRLFRIEND AND 1 SPLIT UP. SHE WANTED TO GET MARRIED, AND 1 DIDN'T WANT HER TO.'

Barbara's Story

'We met for the first time in George Square in Glasgow. It was a blind date along with my friend Joan. We were meeting up with Willie and his pal Rob. It was a Saturday afternoon and Glasgow was grey, still and drizzly. I had not been through from Edinburgh to Glasgow for a number of years. My impression was always of high winds, driving rain, and a city peopled with maniacs talking in badly dubbed English. Although the day was drab the skies suddenly lightened when I set eyes on Rob. Even if he was Glaswegian I wanted him. I was hooked and he was booked.'

♥ 'WILL YOU MARRY ME?'
'NO, BUT I'LL ALWAYS ADMIRE YOUR GOOD TASTE.'

Jane's Story

'I just love those speed dating sessions. There's a nervous sense of mystery and wonder connected to the whole thing: you never know what you are going to go home with. I got a date with my number one, George. I remember when we met up outside this restaurant. There he stood, looking quite nice, clueless to the fact I had already decided we would marry!'

♥ A LITTLE INCOMPATIBILITY IN RELATIONSHIPS IS THE SPICE OF LIFE, PROVIDED THE MAN HAS THE INCOME AND THE WOMAN IS PATIBLE.

David's Story

'Actually, I first saw Debbie when she was sitting in the front row of the King's Theatre as I queued for ice cream at the interval. I thought, "Hey, what a gorgeous creature." Then a few days later I discovered she worked in the company next to the one I worked for. It was another month or so before we actually spoke. I forget what I said, no doubt stumbled over some stupid words, but she was very kind and gracious, and now we are an item.'

A KISS WITHOUT A HUG IS LIKE A FLOWER WITHOUT ITS PERFUME.

If nothing else seems to be working you may want to try a personal advert in a newspaper. Just watch what you are doing: 'Gorgeous Hunk Wishes to Meet You. I am large framed [obese], handsome [self-deluding pathological liar], emotionally secure [just out of Barlinnie], open minded [nobody else will have me], fun loving [an absolute pain in the neck], late 30s [get my bus pass soon], economically viable [once you give me a loan], have own transport [I really should pump up the tyres on my old bike].'

Chapter Two: Winchin'!

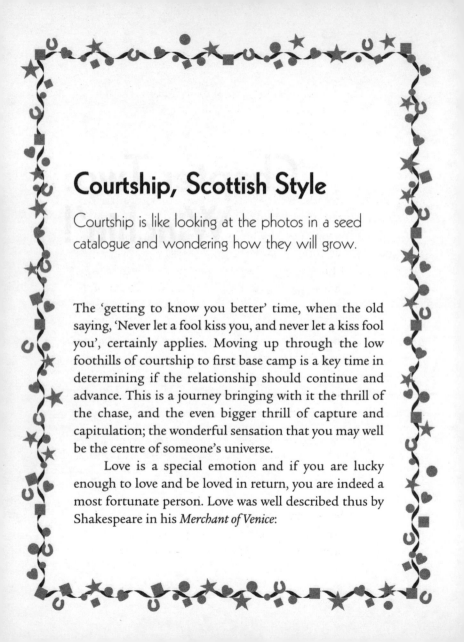

Courtship, Scottish Style

Courtship is like looking at the photos in a seed catalogue and wondering how they will grow.

The 'getting to know you better' time, when the old saying, 'Never let a fool kiss you, and never let a kiss fool you', certainly applies. Moving up through the low foothills of courtship to first base camp is a key time in determining if the relationship should continue and advance. This is a journey bringing with it the thrill of the chase, and the even bigger thrill of capture and capitulation; the wonderful sensation that you may well be the centre of someone's universe.

Love is a special emotion and if you are lucky enough to love and be loved in return, you are indeed a most fortunate person. Love was well described thus by Shakespeare in his *Merchant of Venice*:

Love ever gives, forgives, outlives.
Ever stands with open hands.
And while it lives, it gives
For this is love's prerogative,
To give and give and give.

So how do you know he is the one for you? Easy: he loves you just the way you are; he tickles you pink; he is generous with his time and money; life is brighter when you are with him; you wake up feeling happy when you think of him; he gets the thumbs-up from your family, friends, and even his wee Westie doesn't bite your hand off; you see his faults but still adore him; he hits all the right buttons with you; he's your rock. Love is certainly an adrenaline rush and a spine-tingling whoosh of endorphins that leads to you walking on air.

And how do you know she's the one for you? Easy, she is the one you think about all the time... and she laughs at your jokes.

SOME WOMEN HAVE A TOUGH TIME ... TRYING TO
PROVE TO A MAN THAT HIS INTENTIONS
ARE SERIOUS.

Alister and Jane's Story

'Alister and I had been stepping out for months, then we fell out. So he wrote me a

letter in which he had
included a poem. "If you
were a flower and I were a
bee, my dearest
Jane you
would
learn
how I
love thee."
I sent him a
reply,   also
with a poem.
"I'd show you
best what I think
of thee, if I were a dog and you were a tree."
Anyway, a couple of months later we got
together again. Then I discovered he was the
jealous type. He asked me if there was anybody
else? So I just told him straight, "Don't be daft,
Alister. Do ye think I would be going out with a
man like you if there were?"'

TWO WOMEN WERE DISCUSSING MEN. ONE SAID, 'SOME
MEN ARE TERRIFIED OF COMMITMENT. WE'D BEEN
LIVING TOGETHER FOR OVER A YEAR SO I JUST GAVE
HIM AN ULTIMATUM. "EITHER YOU TELL ME YOUR
SURNAME OR IT'S ALL OVER."'

Joan and Martin's Story

'I brought Martin back one afternoon to meet my parents. He sat next to the gas fire with his coffee cup rattling in his lap. He was nervous and I felt for him. My mother went out of the room a couple of times to bring in biscuits and the likes, and he struggled to his feet every time she came back into the room. He seemed overawed by my father. Talk about deferential, he would have bowed to him if he could. I could see that my mum and dad quite liked him in a sort of old-fashioned way. My mother told me later that I just sat there with a sardonic smile on my face while I stroked our cat, Peebles. Now that we are wed he is completely different with them. Calls them by their first names and even beats dad at golf.'

♥ HOPEFULLY COURTSHIP LEADING TO MARRIAGE IS A WITTY PROLOGUE TO A SATISFYING MARRIAGE.

Suzanne's Story

'I think I must be a bit of a fusspot because when James showed quite a bit of interest in me I just told him straight, "There are a few things I would need to change about you before I learn to accept you as you are." He looked confused and when I thought about what I had said, so was I. However I am now getting him into shape, shall we say.'

FOR SOME COUPLES COURTSHIP IS FAST AND FURIOUS. HE IS FAST AND SHE IS FURIOUS.

Alex's Story

'I asked my dad whether or not I should marry a girl who could take a joke. My father replied that that was the only kind I would get. This turned out to be incorrect. Anne, who worked at the next desk to me, and I started going out together. I was first attracted to her because she did actually laugh and grin when I came out with a funny. I found out she loved the movies and so do I. The only problem has been that we like different kinds of films. Hers tend to be romantic comedies whereas I tend to go for thrillers. We compromised. One week we went to her choice, the next to mine. It has been mostly wonderful, though we have had the occasional wee tiff. Truthfully, she is beyond my wildest dreams. To this day she still likes my dry sense of humour.'

Elspeth's Story

'My friend Edith was always encouraging me to go out more to meet men. I probably was a bit shy. She always said that if I was waiting for Ewan McGregor to chap my door then I would have a long wait. Eventually Edith invited me to a party at her house and I must admit I made a bit of an effort for it, wearing my favourite black dress and black suede high heels. I was also generous with the lipstick. Edith immediately steered me across her living room to meet this particular man. I didn't get a heart lurch when I saw him, but I did like him.

'His name is Archie and we seemed to talk for ages, probably all night. After a couple of wines I realised that this might just be my Ewan McGregor. Archie emailed me the next day and we met for dinner. He turned out to be a nice, sensitive, caring guy. We went for runs in his car, a drink or two, then eventually a holiday in Florida.

'By this time it was getting serious. One day we even stopped on our way to England and had a kiss under the Kissing Gate at Gretna. My mother and father just loved him. I think they had despaired I would ever meet anybody suitable. In fact they eventually encouraged me to marry him. Little did they know I didn't need any encouragement.'

♥ YOU DON'T MARRY SOMEONE YOU CAN LIVE WITH. YOU MARRY SOMEONE YOU CAN'T LIVE WITHOUT.

Chapter Three: 'Och, Ah suppose we better mak it legal, eh?'

The Proposal: down on one knee, perhaps?

Marriage is when a man gets hooked on his ain line.

> O Mary, will you marry me?
> I cannae live without you;
> If I've to wait anither month,
> I'll gae clean gyte about you.
> I canna get a wink o' sleep,
> For thinkin' on your charms;
> To tell the truth, I'm never pleased
> But when you're in my arms.
>
> A. T. MATHEWS

Living together before marriage is certainly not new in Scotland. Five hundred years ago handfasting was extremely popular. In effect a man and a woman had a trial marriage scheduled to last for a year and a day. To symbolise this they had to make the physical contact of 'hands on fist'. When the time was up they had to either marry or go their separate ways. The alleged reason for handfasting was that in small, rural communities there was a need for the wife to produce a family to assist with the husband's work. In effect handfasting was a trial of fertility so if there was no pregnancy by that point, there was no marriage.

Scotsmen are really timid, frightened creatures. For instance if you sneak up behind them and throw confetti all over them the poor souls get fair flustered. This is particularly true during leap years when the terrified wee laddies seek refuge from predatory females.

Sometimes it may take a bit of hinting to make a man get round to proposing. An innocent Scot (if there is such a thing) took his girlfriend out for a Chinese meal. When asked by the waiter if she would like her rice fried or steamed she replied, 'Thrown!' No messing around there.

When men finally pluck up the courage to ask The Question, then the traditional procedure is to seek consent from the head of her family. Notionally that's her father, but in many cases Mother is in the background prompting the old fellow. In olden days the term for the prospective groom seeking the girl's hand was called 'the speirin'. It involved the father of the potential bride feigning displeasure, thereby making the suitor sweat a bit, before giving his consent, or perhaps otherwise.

Then comes the acceptance, and of course, the all-important engagement ring. Diamonds are a girl's best friend and a dog is man's best friend, so now you know which sex has more sense. Diamond engagement rings are based on the belief that the diamond was created from the flames of love.

So how much should these flames of love cost? Some can be flaming expensive. Is it to be a half a carat, one carat or three carat piece of ice? Traditionally, it was generally accepted it should cost two months of a man's salary. Nowadays, well, anything goes. Men, if they have any sense, and most don't, will visit the jeweller of their choice in advance and agree the tray of rings which his fiancée will be shown.

It used to be considered unlucky if the engagement and wedding rings were procured at the same time. What is essential is that the wedding rings are worn on the fourth finger of the left hand. This is due to the Romans believing that the vein in the fourth finger runs directly to the heart. Trust those romantic Italians.

Then again some couples go for his 'n' hers tattoos. Dangerous, if the engagement doesn't work out. Then you have to go around looking for someone of the same name ... unless the tattoo is located in an interesting, discreet place.

When proposals of marriage are not accepted, the ultimate pain is to be invited to your loved one's wedding to someone else. Remember the song...

> I went to your wedding,
> Although I was dreading
> The thought of seeing you there.
> The organ was playing,
> My poor heart was breaking
> The thought of seeing you there.

Ah well. You just have to content yourself that there are other fish in the sea.

When Should a Wedding Take Place?

Marry when the year is new, always loving,
always true.
When February birds do mate, you may wed
or dread your fate.
If you wed when March winds blow, joy and
sorrow both you'll know.
Marry in April when you can, joy of maiden
and for man.
Marry in the month of May, you will surely
rue the day.
Marry when June roses grow, over land and
sea you'll go.
They who in July do wed, must labour
always for their bread.
Whoever wed in August be, many a change
are sure to see.
Marry in September's shine, your living will
be rich and fine.
If in October you do marry, love will come
and riches tarry.

If you wed in bleak November, lasting joy
you will remember.
When December snows fall fast, marry and
true love will last.

So which month should you pick? The one where you can
get a booking in the hotel of your choice, of course! Five
hundred years ago most people got married in June. There
were two reasons for this. The first was that with June came
better weather. Secondly, it was the custom to have a bath
once a year around this time. Even so, some days after the
bath people were starting to smell again, hence the bride
carrying a fresh bouquet of flowers to hide any body odour.
It is further interesting to note that preparing the large tub
of hot water took a lot of effort. So the man of the house
bathed first in the clean, hot water. He was followed by his
sons, then his wife and daughters, then the baby. By this
time the water was filthy so that it would be difficult to find
someone in it. Hence the saying, 'Don't throw the baby out
with the bath water.'

Jamesina and Frank's Story

'He was just plain useless. We had been going
out for what seemed like years, though actually
it was nine months. I thought he would never ask
me. Then one night he dropped one of his
contact lenses on the floor and was down on his

And while you're down there –

knees looking for the blooming thing. I got so frustrated I just asked him if there was anything he wanted to ask me while he was on his knees. The penny finally dropped and he proposed. I nearly said "no" just to spite him. My mother would have killed me if I had refused because she liked him. Still does. Anyway we are happily married now. Funnily enough he has stopped wearing his contact lenses and reverted to glasses. Says if it wasn't for his contacts we might never have got married. Probably right, too.'

♥ A CHAP FROM INVERNESS WAS POSTED TO A POSITION WITH HIS COMPANY IN HONG KONG. HOWEVER, HE PROMISED HE WOULD WRITE TO HIS GIRLFRIEND EVERY DAY. AFTER TWO YEARS HE RETURNED TO FIND HIS GIRL ENGAGED TO THE POSTMAN.

Brian and Amber's Story

'Some men need a jump start. It wis me that suggested we goat merrit otherwise he wid never have goat roon tae it. We had been livin' the gither fur a while so I jist told him ah fancied that "special bit o' paper". "Aye, okay," he said. Talk about romantic!'

♥ THE GLASWEGIAN TOLD HIS PAL THAT THE GIRL HE HAD BEEN DATING HAD REJECTED HIS PROPOSAL OF MARRIAGE. HIS FRIEND EXPLAINED THAT HE SHOULDN'T BE WORRIED AS SOMETIMES A WOMAN'S 'NO' ACTUALLY MEANS 'YES'. 'THE TROUBLE IS,' SAID THE FELLOW,' SHE DIDN'T SAY "NO". WHIT SHE DID WAS LAUGH AND SAY, "HEY, BEAT IT, PAL!"'.

Tony and Jackie's Story

'After dinner we went along to Princes Street for the Hogmanay Party. It was raining a wee bit and quite cold. After the bells, and once the fireworks and music had stopped, Tony went on one knee right into a puddle, and with thousands of people around him almost shouted a proposal.

'I immediately accepted and we went home to tell my parents. He phoned his. The only thing was that my mother got mad at Tony because it took him two months to save up for the ring, and she wanted me to show it off at the staff St Valentine's Ball.'

❤ STEALING A KISS SOMETIMES LEADS TO MARRIAGE; A PERFECT EXAMPLE OF CRIME AND PUNISHMENT.

Paul and Bernie's Story

'I had thought about marriage, especially the "richer or poorer, in sickness and health, till death us do part" bit, for quite a while. Bernie was in bed with tonsillitis at the time and I went to see her with some flowers. It had taken me weeks to get myself all geared up for this even though I was pretty sure she would accept my proposal.

'I went down on one knee beside her bed, held her hand, looked into her eyes and asked, "Bernie, darling, will you marry me?" Says she, "I'll maybe think about it." I was deflated, angry, so I just told her I was going away to climb Munros in Skye with my mate the following day. At this she pipes up and says, "Be careful. I don't want to be considered a widow before we even get married."

'So I just replied, "Listen, it sounds as though we are probably going to get divorced before we get married." That did it. She said, "Of course I'll marry you." I have yet to see Skye never mind climb a mountain there.'

LET'S BE ONE!
ONE LOOK.
ONE SMILE.
ONE TOUCH.
ONE EMBRACE.
ONE KISS.
ONE LOVE.
TWO PEOPLE.
TWO MINDS.
TWO DESTINIES.
ONE ROAD.
ONE JOURNEY.
ONE HAPPY ENDING.
TWOGETHER!

Chapter Four:
Bannockburn
or Culloden?

Scottish Battles on the Road to Bliss

Never pick a first mate with a captain who takes the wind oot o' yer sails.

There can be a few potential battles on the road to marriage. One is the meeting of both sets of the opposition. As Romeo and Juliet found out, marriage is not only about two people falling in love, it's about families, and nowadays some families may have fragmented and reconfigured. When the official asks, 'Who gives this woman in marriage?' quite a number of folks could reply, 'I do.'

Where does such a meeting take place? Neutral ground or for tea, 'suppah' or drinks in one set of parents' house. Then both lots can sit sizing each other up. And have the parents a lot in common apart from their offspring being keen to copulate legally?

Mothers-in-law have been the butt of jokes for

centuries. Are you going to be landed with the control-freak, mother-in-law from hell or are you going to get on well with her? Both parties certainly need to make an effort. The best relationships are ones where good communication, understanding and respect are established early between the families concerned.

And what happens when east meets west and there is a clash of cultures? The rivalry between Edinburgh and Glasgow has gone on over the years and no doubt will continue indefinitely. The citizens of both cities have opinions on the other, but it is clear that they have more in common than they have differences.

A BACHELOR IS MERELY A GROOM IN TRAINING.

'Who gives this woman...?'

Nowadays it is expected that both parties to a marriage should share the chores at home. It is important to try to find a husband who is prepared to help around the house, who cooks from time to time, who helps with the cleaning and who has a good job. So, perhaps the girl  should really select a man from Edinburgh. However, it is important to find a husband with a sense of humour, in which case you should really select a man from Glasgow. This, of course, is all just nonsense as the real test is the character of the man himself.

On this very theme, if you wish to stay away from trouble during weddings, it is better not to allude to where individuals come from, or make inappropriate jokes and impromptu observations. At the wedding of James from Edinburgh and Catherine from Glasgow, the bride's father told a couple of rather lame jokes and then stated, 'Where in this life would we be without laughter?' Someone shouted, 'Edinburgh!' The groom's mother's face was a picture.

In a not dissimilar vein, a foolish bridegroom observed in his wedding speech that he had heard of a contest where the first prize was a week in Glasgow, the second prize was two weeks in Glasgow, and the third prize three weeks in Glasgow.

Then his throwaway line was that he once spent a weekend in Glasgow one day. Apparently he is still alive.

The story goes that a lovely lass from Perth had three suitors: one from Edinburgh, one from Aberdeen and one from Glasgow. They all asked her father for her hand in marriage. The father determined to give them a test. He put a cabbage, a potato and a knife on a table and asked them to identify the odd one out. The fellow from Edinburgh selected the knife because the other two were edible. The Aberdonian agreed it was the knife, but insisted it was because the cabbage and the potato are vegetable and the knife is mineral. The Glaswegian, however, insisted that the odd one out was the cabbage. 'The cabbage?' queried the girl's father. 'Aye,' replied the Glaswegian. 'Sure ye can make chips wi' the other two!' We can only guess at which suitor was successful.

SOME MEN BELIEVE IN LIFE, LIBERTY AND
THE HAPPINESS OF PURSUIT.

If a Scot is marrying someone who is English, it's really much better to keep away from any 'Sassenach observations', however tempted you are at the wedding. Many Scots have married into English families and vice versa, so the old jokes and digs are best forgotten.

Another potential hazard on the road to married bliss, especially in the west of Scotland, is the so-called, 'mixed marriage' where that line from the old song, 'Goin' to the chapel and we're gonna get married', may have other connotations. The real problem with mixed marriages is not that one is Catholic and the other Protestant. The trouble is that one is a man and the other a woman. That's the real rub.

A young couple started dating, but she was soon under pressure from her parents as he was not a Roman Catholic. So she invited him along to her church, gave him literature to read and got him to attend instruction classes. One day her parents found her sobbing uncontrollably. She explained that he now wanted to become a priest.

Yvonne's Story

'I can remember standing at the windae of a night, patiently waiting for my handsome honey of a boyfriend to arrive in his red TR7. All the while ma faither waid be askin',

"Whaurs's yon holy terror? Is his Popemobile no' here yet, hen?"'

♥ REGARDLESS OF ALL OTHER CONSIDERATIONS, ALWAYS GO FOR THE GUY WHO TURNS AROUND ONE LAST TIME WHEN YOU PART.

Of course there are other kinds of mixed marriages. For instance, it could be a marriage between a lawyer and a human being.

Chapter Five:
'Gift list or no gift list, that is the question'

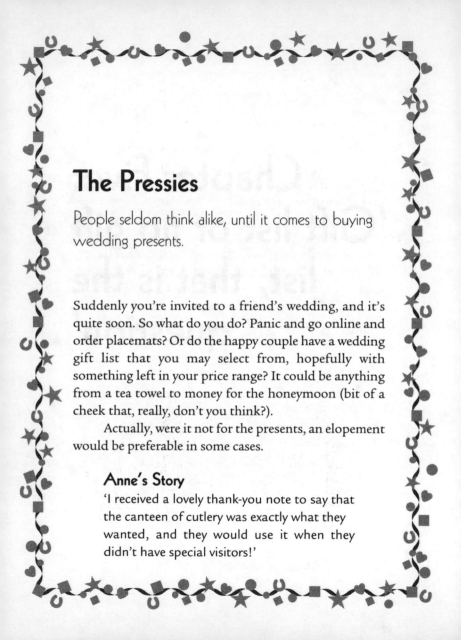

The Pressies

People seldom think alike, until it comes to buying wedding presents.

Suddenly you're invited to a friend's wedding, and it's quite soon. So what do you do? Panic and go online and order placemats? Or do the happy couple have a wedding gift list that you may select from, hopefully with something left in your price range? It could be anything from a tea towel to money for the honeymoon (bit of a cheek that, really, don't you think?).

Actually, were it not for the presents, an elopement would be preferable in some cases.

Anne's Story
'I received a lovely thank-you note to say that the canteen of cutlery was exactly what they wanted, and they would use it when they didn't have special visitors!'

'IN MARRIAGE THE BRIDE GETS A SHOWER,
BUT FOR THE GROOM IT'S CURTAINS.

A shrewd Aberdeen businessman made sure that he only invited married couples as guests to his wedding. The idea was that if you only invite married people, all the presents will be clear profit, with no further outlay for their future nuptials. Until the second weddings come around, that is...

So will you cringe with embarrassment at the thought of asking aunts and uncles, whom you haven't seen since you passed them a plate of sausage rolls at Granny's funeral tea, for a top-of-the-range dinner service or a flat-screen HD telly? At least with a present list you ensure no duplicate or unwanted gifts will clutter up your bottom drawer. Or are you going to leave it open so

Show of Gifts

that guests will be free to buy anything they choose? Do you really want a blue silk-lined box of six silver-plated, fruit knives with unusual designs on their bone handles, in order that it can sit in the darkest recess of your attic?

Or perhaps six rice cookers and steamers, five picture frames, four lamps, three duvet covers, two toasters and enough wine glasses, probably all from IKEA, to start a fashionable deli in Broughty Ferry.

Some brides-to-be still have 'Shows of Presents'. This ensures the neighbours compete to be the giver of the best present. If you live in an apartment block you are laughing. Anyway, what are you going to do with all this booty? Will your local charity shop end up as the real beneficiary?

LOVE IS A FLOWER. MARRIAGE IS A TREE TO
SHELTER IT UNDER.

Perhaps you have been living together for quite a while and in reality have most items anyway? You could then decide to upgrade your furnishings or opt for some charity gifts to be sent to needy people in the third world. A couple of goats or a well of clean water? A bit different from the wedding china your mother got thirty-five years ago, huh? You may even consider opting for the presence of your guests rather than their presents.

MARRIAGE TURNS NIGHT OWLS INTO
HOMING PIGEONS.

Chapter Six:
The Preparations

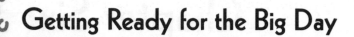

Getting Ready for the Big Day

The best laid schemes o' mice and men gang
aft agley.

Planning a wedding can be stressful. The coming together
of diverse ideas from two families is never easy. It's a ritual
as old as marriage itself. A wedding is the culmination of
months of fun, laughter, chaos and occasional setbacks.
There are so many variations to be considered. Is it to be a
traditional, religious, white wedding with a huge bash
afterwards; a pink, girly, all-singing, all-dancing affair, a civil
ceremony or a commitment ceremony?

The rigmarole, the whole kit-and-caboodle, the
attendant hoopla, the minutiae of wedding detail is
endless... and expensive. In other words there are a
thousand and one things to consider (see the glossary at
the back of the book).

And the main question is: whose savings account is
taking the hit? Is it the bride's father, or, with many couples

now already established in a relationship, the couple themselves? The answer to this question will also determine the balance of power in decision-making. Most critically, it may determine how many tables are reserved for friends and distant relatives of the parents.

Under the Marriage (Scotland) Act 2002, it is now possible for civil marriages to be solemnised in various places approved by local authorities. By Scottish law, both parties to a proposed civil or religious marriage are required to submit marriage notice forms to the registrar of the district in which the marriage is to take place. This notice must be given in the three-month period prior to the date of the marriage and not later than fifteen days before that date.

The Overseas Wedding Option

Perhaps the big decision has been made to have your wedding abroad; pledging your vows while bathed in warm sunshine in paradise. Of course your honeymoon then starts immediately: you are there. It can be tempting to leave behind Scotland's unpredictable weather and tie the knot beside a blue sea, under exotic lofty palms. Beats drizzle and midges, though watch out for mozzies and falling coconuts.

So, what's it to be? Italy, Turkey, Greece, the

Maldives, Jamaica, Barbados, South America or Australia? Perhaps a wedding while on safari, or barefoot listening to a Polynesian choir on a beach in the South Pacific? (Please note that 'Flower o' Scotland' is unlikely to be included in their repertoire.) The list of destinations is endless. Mind you, East Kilbride, Arbroath and Dingwall have their own unique charms, too. Will you feel a wee bit guilty at leaving your homeland behind as you stand in the Graceland Storybook Chapel in Las Vegas with Elvis singing three songs of your choice? Would you have liked your old Auntie Mabel to be there? It is all up to you. Yes, love encircles the world and whether at home or abroad you will want a world-class wedding.

Civil Partnerships and Celebrations of Commitment for same-sex couples are now also popular in a number of countries, with Canada offering full marriage equality to same-sex couples.

Enid's Story

'We opted to have our wedding in St Lucia. Brian and I plus my bridesmaid and our best man flew out there. It was fabulous. The beaches were just wonderful. My mother had told Brian that he should take plenty of photographs, and not just of the wedding (we got one of the guests staying at the hotel to take them – he was actually a guy from Leith).

Anyway, my mother had also said that as they get fabulous sunsets in the West Indies we should try and capture a sunset as one of our wedding photo collection. Needless to say we forgot all about the sunset. When we got back home and looked at our set of photos, there was no sunset. Brian then took a couple of photos

'I gather it's sunny in Scotland.'

of a sunset over Bute. When my mother saw the complete set of photos she commented, "Aye, you don't get sunsets like that in Scotland."'

Invitations

Who will be the bridesmaids and the best man, and which guests are you going to invite? Do you send out advance notifications in the form of 'Save-the-Date' cards prior to the actual invites? And remember, if you want most invitees to accept your invitation, there are two key words which should go on the invitation card: Open bar!

Do you invite ex-boyfriends, ex-girlfriends, even ex-spouses? And what about the conundrum of your mother's first and third husbands? What about suckling babies, nieces and nephews. Will it be a child-free wedding reception? Then there's the cousin on your father's side that you haven't seen since the last family funeral, and that was ten years ago, but who is at present out on good behaviour. The list of permutations and hidden tensions is endless. It's a minefield.

♥ MARRIED LIFE MAY WELL BE EASIER THAN
PLANNING THE WEDDING.

Rosie's Story

'I wanted a big wedding as we have a lot of very close relations and family friends but Raymond wanted a quiet affair, just a small coterie of friends. Needless to say we had a big wedding. Anyway, my dad was paying, so that was that. We never ever thought that planning a wedding could be so time consuming. So many wee details like colour schemes for tables etc. Talk about a logistical challenge. It became very clear early on that men and women have a radically different approach to weddings. Women want everything to be absolutely perfect, from the wedding dress to the type of wine served. As for Raymond, I think he would have been quite happy to have found an old suit at the Glasgow Barras, and got the minister to marry us at the nineteenth hole of his golf club.'

MARRIAGE IS THE ONGOING EXPERIENCE OF GETTING USED TO THINGS YOU HADN'T EXPECTED.

Who Does What on the Day?

Groom Turns up on the big day, reasonably sober, and gives himself up now his probation period is over.
Bride Looks lovely, smiles, and grabs him before he changes his mind.

Bride's father Hands her over to another guy to continue keeping her in the manner to which she would like to become accustomed.

Bride's mother Develops a crick in the neck from her critical appraisal of the groom's mum's get-up.

Official/Minister/Priest Turns up on the big day to prompt the couple with their lines.

Best man Ensures the shaky groom is ready on time at the starting line, looks after the rings, and mortifies the parents with his revelations after dinner.

Bridesmaid Reassures the bride, tries to either pull or fend off the best man, and finishes the evening scrummaging for the bouquet.

I dreamed of a wedding of style and taste,
A church filled with family and friends.
I asked him what kind of wedding he
          wanted,
He just said, one to make me his wife.

Chapter Seven: Hen and stag nights/weekends!

Last Days of Freedom

A guid nicht oot fur the lads an' lassies means a drookit heid in the morn.

Hen Dos – Girls Just Wanna Have Fun!

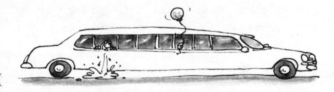

Hen dos invariably feature leaving your inhibitions behind, wearing flashing L-plates, drinking copious cocktails, being driven in pink stretch limos and meeting up with naked muscle-bound men covered in baby oil. Or it can be groups of lassies flying to Benidorm providing apparently obligatory outbreaks of 'Viva España' and 'Here Come the Girls' whilst wearing T-shirts their mothers wouldn't approve of such as:

I'm a virgin from Dundee. This is an old T-shirt.
Good girls go to heaven. Bad girls go to Spain.
Miss Naughty seeks Mr Naughty.
If found return to Hen Party.
Hens on the Run.
Loose Women Tour of Malaga.
I'm She who must be Obeyed. Give us a kiss!
Bridesmaids Revisited.

Usually a theme for a do is agreed by all the hens themselves. Perhaps they all fancy themselves as nurses, bunny girls with fluffy tails, cowgirls, trolley dollies or even angels with wings (totally inappropriate for naughty hen dos!). Then it's on with the Girls' Nite Out hats, the BadGirl garters, Devil horns and Naughty Ladies' wands, and off in search of good-natured nonsense.

Sheena's Story

'One of the bridesmaids organised what she called a sketching party. "Trust me," she said. All fifteen of us arrived at this so-called studio, were given paper and crayons, plus glasses of white wine. In came two male models (hunks), totally starkers. They posed for us for half an hour, then the idea was that they would judge our efforts. Still naked, they came round and examined our drawings and made some naughty remarks. By this time we all had at least three glasses of wine in us and the whole thing was a scream. Shall we say that some of the girls became a little "adventurous".'

♥ WATCH OUT FOR THE GUY WHO IS FOOTLOOSE AND FIANCÉE-FREE.

Kate's Story

'We just decided to do a pub crawl around Aberdeen's more lively hostelries. We all wore ridiculous T-shirts saying "Hen Night, no cocks allowed".

'It was probably in the third pub that someone had the bright idea we should buy another present for the bride by "selling kisses" to members of the opposite sex. One of the girls made over £20 and ended up meeting a guy who is now her partner.'

♥ BEFORE MARRIAGE, A MAN YEARNS FOR THE WOMAN HE LOVES. AFTER MARRIAGE, THE 'Y' DISAPPEARS.

Sylvia's Story

'The theme for our hen weekend in Majorca was Itsy Bitsy Teenie Weenie Yellow Polka Dot

Bikini. All eighteen of us bought yellow bikinis, even wearing them on the plane (over our clothes). At the resort we went around all the time wearing them.

'Some of my friends are somewhat overweight, and their bikinis were challenged, to put it mildly. It was all great fun.'

♥ ONLY LAZY PEOPLE THROW KISSES.

Morag's Story

'We hired the village hall for my hen night. The main feature was the "boat-race", a speed-drinking contest. Chairs were placed around the floor and everyone had to stand on them holding the alcoholic drink of their choice.

'You had to drink the whole lot down then jump on to the next chair. Your glass was then refilled and the process started again. All the other guests were standing around cheering on this activity. The winner, the one still left standing on her chair, was Irene, a skinny wee soul who must have gone through quite a bit of drink.

'She was presented with a bottle of something or other as the Speed Drinker of the

Year. Then she and her friend left early saying they were going to the pub for a drink!'

 ROMANCE IS THE ICING, BUT LOVE IS THE CAKE.

Pat's Story

'There were sixteen of us and we hired a BoogieBus. I told the girls to "dress to kill". One of them said she was dressed as Rose West! Two came as Bonnie and Clyde. The whole thing was just crazy. The bus had everything: wraparound-luxury seating, karaoke, lasers, strobes, mirrors on the ceiling with stars. We stopped at three well-known pubs plus a nightclub. At the end we all got poured off the BoogieBus while singing our hearts out. What a night!'

 MARRIAGE IS FANTASTIC IN THAT IT PROVIDES PLENTY OF TEMPTATION AND PLENTY OF OPPORTUNITY, AND IT'S ALL ABOVE BOARD.

Stag Nights – Men Behaving Badly!

Many Scottish males declare before they get hitched that they will be the master of their own home or they will know the reason why. After marriage they know the reason why.

However the Scottish male can always console himself with the thought of the stag do; the glorious hours of raucous freedom before the bedroom door finally slams shut. Traditionally the stag night is also meant to reassure the groom's friends that although he will marry they will still remain part of his life.

So what kind of stag do is it going to be? A wild one, a very wild one, or an outrageously wild one? Just one wee bit of warning: make sure you do not offend the local authorities if your event is abroad.

T-shirts for the boys may be along the lines of:

The game is over for him, but not for me!
I'm Best Man. Are you my Best Woman?
This is the night before the morning after.
Probably the best lover in the world.

What about a little bungee jumping to start with? After all, the poor groom is shortly going to be at the end of his tether. Or it could be some bird watching, and not of the feathered kind. Or even being undressed by two strippers in a club. Naughty, naughty! However, do make sure you do something that the stag will really find fun. Not too embarrassing. Aye, that'll be right!

'I'm getting married in the morning' may not be accurate for many stag and hen nights. It may be some days prior to the main event. The general opinion is that the stag do should not be on the night prior to the wedding. Brides and their mothers are not impressed with comatose grooms suffering after a night on the tiles.

Stag dos can test the male's human endurance, and sometimes friendships, to the limit. The problem is that boys will be boys, and they just love to get up to all types of malarkey. They may well set out with razzle-dazzle braces, Afro wigs and good intentions, then the demon drink intervenes and before you know it, grooms end up with their eyebrows shaved, or find themselves tied or super-glued to a lamppost, covered in peanut butter.

It has not been unknown for best men to arrange stag nights to take place at the same venue as a wild hen night. In such cases anything can happen. Or depending on the personality and interests of the groom it could be a casino visit, a golf competition, a fishing competition, a booze cruise, a walk up the West Highland Way, a Munro climb, a paint-balling session, or just a meal out with the lads.

Dickie's Story

'You may well know that in many of the agricultural areas of Scotland the stag tradition is "The Blackening", right? Well, I made all my friends swear they wouldn't do this. I told them that it would upset my elderly mother.

In the pub the night before my stag I had the horrible feeling I was about to be abducted, so I ran outside, jumped in my car, locked the doors, started up, only to discover the wheels had been removed. I was caught, stripped, blackened, and paraded round the pubs in Angus for the next twelve hours!'

💜 'LOVE IS BLIND – THAT'S WHY LOVERS LIKE TO TOUCH.

Brian's Story

'I had my stag in Budapest. We all went to a strip joint where the main feature was that for about £100 someone could remove their clothes and join a stripper in a sort of glass cubicle on stage. All the boys chipped in some money, and I had a great time on stage with this gorgeous creature. It was so good that my best man (we called him Bilbo Baggins as he was "The Keeper of the Ring") produced £100, stripped off his kit, and was soon to be seen cavorting (a polite word for it) with another stripper in the cubicle.'

💜 'BREATHES THERE A MAN WITH SOUL SO DEAD, WHO NEVER TO HIS WIFE HAS SAID, 'FORGET BREAKFAST, COME BACK TO BED.'

George's Story

'On my stag night in Glasgow the boys had brought along a ball and chain which was attached to my leg. After a few hours spent visiting various pubs we ended up in Glasgow Central station. The drunken fools were going to tie me up and put me in the toilet of the overnight sleeper to London. The wedding was the next day for heaven's sake! In the end I am pleased to say they bottled out.'

 IN LOVE, ONE AND ONE ADD UP TO ONE.

Eric's Story

'At the end of the stag night the boys "boot-polished" me and here was I going commando under my kilt. At least by the end of the honeymoon I had lost most of my shine!

 MARRIAGE IS NOT A NOUN BUT A VERB. IT ISN'T SOMETHING YOU GET. IT'S SOMETHING YOU DO.

Jake's Story

'It was a great stag night. I drank twelve pints of Bass, four Bacardis and a few whiskies, as far as I can remember. Best stag night I've ever been to. I crawled to bed, and with throbbing head and deep breaths gnawed at the edge of the sheet, until sleep overtook me about two minutes later.

'Next day, at the wedding, if I had been peely-wally that would have been acceptable.

'My father told me I looked like a cadaver on electric soup.'

💙 TRUE LOVE IS SMILING AT EACH OTHER, AND MEANING IT.

Ross's Story

'Eight of us boys jetted off to Vegas. What a wild time we had. I don't remember sleeping the whole time. Just on the plane back. I dressed as Elvis (white Vegas comeback suit, of course) and the rest of the gang were dressed as security guards, black uniform, shades, earpieces, the lot. It was amazing the number of people who stopped us looking for autographs, and the number of women who approached us! Wow, I nearly cancelled the wedding and stayed on in the City of Sin. Funnily enough I have been back in Vegas for another stag. This time the groom dressed as Batman and the rest of us were Robins.'

💙 A MARRIAGE IS LIKE HAGGIS. ONLY THOSE RESPONSIBLE FOR IT KNOW WHAT GOES INTO IT.

Simon's Story

'Being a big fan of the film *Top Gun* I hired a cinema for a private showing for all my friends.

'The cinema came up trumps and actually changed their electronic sign outside to say, "Simon stars in *Top Gun*"! We all dressed up in flight gear and posed for photographs outside the cinema for the local newspaper.'

♥ AFTER AN EXHAUSTING WEDDING DAY, THE BRIDE AND GROOM WERE FINALLY ALONE. 'MAY I KISS YOU, DARLING?' HE ASKED. 'OH HEAVENS,' SHE EXCLAIMED. 'NOT ANOTHER AMATEUR!'

Chapter Eight: Getting knotted!

The Wedding Day

The culmination of love is when you write your first name with his last.

> Fy, let us a' to the wedding,
> For they will be lilting there;
> For Jock's to be married to Maggy,
> The lass wi' the golden hair.

J. BAILLIE

Your wedding day is a once-in-a-lifetime experience, an unforgettable moment, a gateway to the future as you celebrate your seal of love and make a commitment to each other before you start your life together. So plan not just to survive it but to enjoy it. Well, that's the theory anyway.

The fundamental rule for the couple, on this happiest of days, is that the groom must not see his doe-eyed bride-to-be before they meet at the altar. It is also the time the officiating person gives the blushing bride something to wrap around her little finger, besides the groom. It is a time when people cry, especially bank managers.

Marriage is an investment that pays dividends if you pay interest. It is also a sort of graduation ceremony in which the man loses his Bachelor's Degree without acquiring a Master's.

honeymoon luggage

MOST WEDDINGS ARE HAPPY. IT'S THE TRYING TO
LIVE TOGETHER AFTERWARDS THAT CAUSES ALL
THE PROBLEMS.

Chloe's Story

'The morning of the day before the wedding I phoned to make sure our transport arrangements were okay, especially the white limo we had booked. I spoke to the chap who owns the company. He said, "Aye, ah wis jist thinkin' o' phonin' ye the nicht. Unfortunately the limo's clutch has gone and the other motor ye ordered has failed its MOT. Sorry ah cannae help ye at yer waddin', hen." I just about went spare!

'Then I phoned around and managed to get a couple of white taxis. I was fair fizzing, I can tell you. You know how the song says that love and marriage go together like a horse and carriage – well, we nearly had a horse and an old cart.'

♥ LOVE WASN'T PUT IN YOUR HEART TO STAY.
LOVE ISN'T LOVE TILL YOU GIVE IT AWAY.

Andy and Tina's Story

'Our wedding car was an ancient Rolls. Lovely to look at but it did pong a bit inside. Two hundred yards from the church the bleedin' thing stopped. Just wouldn't start. I was already fifteen minutes late, so as it was a nice day and I didn't want Andy to change his mind, I just hopped out and my father and I sort of ran to the church. After the ceremony the Rolls was fixed and waiting to take Andy and I to the reception. Two hundred yards from the hotel it broke down again. Andy was getting mad but the driver said that there would be no charge. To this day Andy still talks about that car. He christened it Flattery because it got us nowhere!'

♥ YOU CAN'T WRAP LOVE IN A BOX.
BUT YOU CAN WRAP YOUR LOVER IN A HUG.

Patrick and Liz's Story

'I think that Patrick and his best man, Mick, had had a wee snifter before the ceremony. We were all standing there listening to the priest droning on, when suddenly Patrick just passed out. After a couple of minutes he seemed to recover and the ceremony continued. All of a sudden Mick keeled over, but came round quite quickly. While we were signing the register, a friend of mine, Joan, sang "Blow the Wind Southerly". Half way through the song she fell backwards! They say that incidents go in threes and I was pleased that the rest of the day went as planned.'

THERE SHOULD BE A NEW BOOK PUBLISHED: 'WOMEN ARE FROM VENUS, MEN ARE WRONG.'

Simon and Pat's Story

'My father and I arrived at the church in non-stop rain. The front path was a mosaic of wee pools. The graveyard was silently filling up with water that couldn't penetrate the soil. All I was conscious of was the swish of passing cars wetting my dress. I squelched up the stairs and into the church. The dress was soaked. A bit of a damp start, but it worked out all right in the end.'

A WIFE HAS MORE POWER OVER HER HUSBAND THAN THE GOVERNMENT.

Peter and Jane's Story

'Peter and I had decided to have an

old-fashioned wedding. We even threw coins out of the taxi after the ceremony. Would you believe it, there were no children around and we threw out a good ten pounds' worth. Never mind, we then sat back in the car and enjoyed a flute of champers.'

♥ THERE IS NO MORE LOVELY, FRIENDLY AND CHARMING
RELATIONSHIP THAN A
GOOD MARRIAGE.

Paul and Liza's Story

'Our best man, Joe, was a cuddly man who was somewhat rotund but had a lovely round, open face. He opted to travel on one of the coaches carrying guests from the church to the hotel. Joe tends to go over the score sometimes. Anyway, for reasons only known to himself, he opted to moon out of the rear window of the coach. Unfortunately for Joe the minister and his wife were travelling in the car directly behind the bus. Later the minister referred to the incident when he was chairing the reception proceedings. However, he graciously said that he didn't know if Joe was mooning or merely looking out of the back window.'

♥ HUSBANDS MAY WEAR THE TROUSERS BUT WIVES CONTROL THE ZIPS.

Archie and Margaret's Story

'During the wedding ceremony, when the minister got to the bit about "With all my worldly goods I thee endow" someone said in a loud whisper, "There goes his laptop."'

♥ A COMPROMISE IS AN ARRANGEMENT BETWEEN HUSBAND AND WIFE WHEREBY THEY AGREE TO LET HER HAVE HER OWN WAY.

Angus and Louise's Story

'The minister was young and clearly nervous. Instead of the usual, "You are now lawfully joined in marriage", he said, "You are now joyfully loined in marriage."'

 A MARRIAGE LICENCE ALLOWS A WOMAN TO DRIVE A MAN.

Gordon and Simone's Story

'The car taking my father and me to the church left a bit to be desired. In fact, at the end of the day we refused to pay. No wonder. When we arrived outside the church the brakes sort of failed and we ran into a taxi parked at the kerbside. My father was going ballistic and I was a bit shaken up myself. Eventually we got into the church and everything else went okay. Actually we had a good laugh about it later on.'

WHAT'S HERS IS HERS AND WHAT'S HIS IS HERS, TOO.

Tim and Betty's Story

'On the way to the Register Office the white ribbon on the limo's bonnet came off, and wrapped itself around a cyclist we were just about to overtake. The poor man went head over heels and we had to stop. The driver used his mobile and called an ambulance. He then took us to the church, dropped us, and went back to the cyclist as the police were also coming. Thankfully when we came out of the church the limo was there, plus the white ribbon. Apparently the cyclist was okay.'

♥ 'MARRIAGE IS THE PROCESS OF FINDING OUT WHAT KIND OF MAN YOUR WIFE WOULD HAVE PREFERRED.

The Wedding Day in Eight Episodes

Episode 1: 'Aw Look, Sure She's Jist Lovely'

The Dress and Hairdos

A SPILLED DRINK ALWAYS FLOWS IN THE DIRECTION OF
THE MOST EXPENSIVE DRESS.

White wedding gowns symbolise purity and joy. A traditional rhyme goes as follows:

> Married in white, you have chosen alright.
> Married in green, ashamed to be seen.
> Married in red, you wish yourself dead.
> Married in blue, you will always be true.
> Married in yellow, ashamed of your fellow.
> Married in black, you will wish yourself back.
> Married in pink. Of you he'll think.

However, today fashion and personal choice dictate the colour. The finery of the bride's trousseau may cost thousands but, who cares, you only get married once and you are going to be looking at photos of it for the rest of your life. So what's it going to be? Perhaps a dress of cream lace adorned with a deeper cream bow on the back or a Cinderella-style off-the-shoulder gown? A full-length, antique lace veil, all flowing behind you as you're escorted by ten young attendants and umpteen bridesmaids with matching cream dresses, coffee coloured sashes and chaplets of cream flowers in their hair?

Is your wedding dress to be really, really special, only worn once, then hung in a wardrobe for a future daughter to dress up in, or are you going to have this silken creation cut down, dyed and made into a party dress?

Remember that your gown is a key symbol. Your wedding photographs may well be hung on your granddaughter's wall sixty years hence. You therefore want this heavenly work of art to be a timeless item high on the Richter scale of bridal wear, the ultimate dazzling dress in which to rustle down the aisle as you totter along in your Jimmy Choo slippers. Yes, those Choos were made for walkin'!

Tradition may still play a part in the bride's attire. She may opt for 'something old, something new, something borrowed, something blue'. The 'something old' may be a gift from her mother, symbolising the passing on of a mother's wisdom. 'Something new' can be the bride's dress, symbolising the new start to married life. 'Something borrowed' comes from a happily married couple in the hope that something of their married bliss will rub off on the newlyweds. The 'something blue' is said to come from the Roman tradition of the bride having a blue border as a sign of modesty and love. Nowadays this usually takes the form of a blue garter. If you see a bride limping down the aisle then the chances are that she has placed a small silver coin in a shoe to bring good luck to the marriage – or her shoes are too tight!

Just imagine, you stand behind the curtain in a bridal shop. You're strapped into an enormous fluffy, lacy creation by an assistant who tells you that this one is 'just you'. No way; you look like Bridezilla. Outside the cubicle curtain the judge and jury waits, sipping complimentary coffees. No doubt it comprises your mother plus two of your best friends, ready to pronounce a verdict on you, Wedding Barbie, dressed in your 'blancmange'.

Then you step out from the cubicle and let the jury deliver their verdict. Will they oooh and aaah? No! Juries can be so unfair, cruel and come to the wrong conclusion. They not only give it the thumbs down – they laugh! You're hurt to the quick, whip off the veil and sob before asking the vital question, 'Is it because my bum looks big in this?'

Don't worry. There will be another 'white puffball' produced any minute by your wedding design assistant. They want a satisfied customer to hoof it down the aisle in one of their meringues, even if the creation does looks like a large curtain unsuccessfully trying to cover your décolletage. Just don't select one that starts late and ends early, for although we may live in a nuclear age you certainly don't want to have fallout on the big day.

Or you may want to take a radically different approach, and opt for a vintage wedding dress and satin slippers, perhaps even found in your local charity shop. At least this would save your credit card from squeaking like a stuck pig under the unexpected pressure.

Whatever your choice of wedding attire, most brides would rather draw a veil over its cost. When it comes to veils and headdresses, there are plenty of options. Many brides choose tiaras nowadays, with or without a veil, though others prefer a 'crown' of real or silk flowers. Veils tend to be symbolic. As the ceremony begins, the chief bridesmaid lifts back the veil, in order that the man can ensure he has not been landed with a ringer. Anyway, as Granny used to say, *a bonny face would suit a dish cloot*! A hat may be preferred, especially if the wedding dress is not a traditional one. Some prefer dresses or suits reminiscent of period riding gear, worn with a 'riding hat', all in ivory or white.

Then there's the hair treatment. All brides pray for a dry day with little wind. Unfortunately sometimes the velocity of the wind is directly proportional to the price of the hairdo. It is reasonable to assume that Murphy's Law will probably kick in at some stage, to guarantee the precious preparations will be affected by the elements. It's here that the bridesmaids play a vital part in ensuring that their charge always looks her very best, regardless of fate.

Jumping out of an aircraft at ten thousand feet, with the best man handing over the ring at five thousand feet, is not to be recommended for brides who have spent money

and time on that special hairdo. Perhaps a ceremony on a quiet cruise boat on Loch Lomond may just about keep the hair in some sort of order.

And what about the finery of the poor groom? What gear will he appear in? Will it be the splendour of a swinging kilt, perhaps a Grey Spirit or the Loch Lomond, or will it be morning wear, such as a Prince Edward outfit with a top hat. The bride may have to give him a bit of advice here, just as she has doubtless done all along.

Then there is the problem of headgear and social kissing at weddings. Traditionally, lady guests wearing hats do not remove their hats until after the wedding breakfast. Consequently, until that point the mothers of the bride and groom, and possibly a hatted bride, may have to conduct all their 'mwah-mwah' moments with their hats on. An over-large brim may oblige 'air-kissing' – quite a fashionable technique during pandemics.

Episode 2: 'Here Comes the Bride, Sixty Inches Wide!'

The Wedding Music: Odes to Joy

Wedding music is important. It can create the perfect romantic mood and leave the guests appropriately entertained during such times as the signing of the register. A religious ceremony traditionally has live musicians playing: an organist, choir or string quartet. A civil ceremony may either have live music or perhaps an appropriate CD. Indeed, some special piece can have a resonance which continues to reverberate even after the wedding is over.

The popular choices are usually along the lines of: 'Air on a G String' by J. S. Bach; 'The Bridal Chorus' ('Here Comes the Bride') by Richard Wagner; The 'Romeo and Juliet' love theme by Tchaikovsky; Mozart's 'Wedding March'; 'Triumphal March' by Grieg; 'Ave Maria' by Schubert and Beethoven's 'Ode To Joy'.

Some Scottish couples, depending on the venue, opt for something different. The Beatles's 'She Loves You' is popular. Other favourites are 'Take My Breath Away' from the film *Top Gun*, the soundtracks from *Braveheart* and *What a Wonderful World*. Also Sonny and Cher's 'I Got you Babe', Elton John's 'Can You Feel the Love Tonight', Madonna's 'Crazy for You', Extreme's 'More Than Words' or Nat King Cole's 'When I Fall in Love'.

Not recommended are 'Fight the Good Fight with All Thy Might' and 'The Lady Is a Tramp'.

During the signing of the register someone singing The Waterboys' 'How Long Will I Love You' is popular, because of the lyrics. It can also be used as part of the bridegroom's speech.

An Organist's Story

'I had played for an hour and the bride had not appeared. A hurried phone call to the bride's home elicited the following: "She's still daein' her herr." "Well," I said, "just tell her that if she is not here in ten minutes, herr or no herr, I'm going home with my fee!"'

MARRIAGE IS AN ADVENTURE; MIND YOU SO IS GOING OVER NIAGARA FALLS IN A BARREL.

Another Organist's Story

'The bride phoned me to tell me she wanted to come down the aisle to the Robin Hood music. I asked her if she was sure about this, but she insisted it meant something special for her. When she and her father started down the aisle I duly played 'Robin Hood, Robin Hood, riding through the glen'. The bride immediately burst into tears. It transpired she had wanted '(Everything I Do) I Do It For You' sung by Bryan Adams in the film *Robin Hood: Prince of Thieves*.'

Here comes the bride,
Sixty inches wide.
Sliding doon the banister
On her big backside.

Here comes the bride,
Fifty inches wide.
Waddlin' up the aisle
With her hips so wide.

Here comes the bride
Forty inches wide.
Sailing doon the aisle
Like a steamer oan the Clyde.

Here comes the bride,
Thirty inches wide.
Starving for wedding cake
She's her slimming club's pride.

Episode 3: 'Do you take this man to be your Awful Wedded Husband?'

Last opportunity to play your 'Get out of Jail Free' card

> 'I AM' IS ONE OF THE SHORTEST SENTENCES IN
> OUR LANGUAGE. 'I DO' IS THE LONGEST.

It's your big moment. The official is in front of you both. The gathering of friends and relations are sitting behind, watching and listening carefully. The women are expectant, mostly smiling, some wiping away a tear. The men are somewhat garrotted by tight new shirt collars. Your expensive silver shoes are crippling you. Then comes the wedding vows with that nerve-racking question put to those gathered, 'Does anyone know of any just cause or lawful impediment why these two people should not be joined in marriage?' This is followed by the inevitable anxious moment and normally welcome silence. We are all still waiting for a cry of 'Aye, she's merrit tae me an' we've goat six weans!'

Try not to have the wedding jitters and fluff your lines when exchanging vows. They may well be recorded for posterity, and future offspring could fall about laughing fifteen years hence.

A somewhat plain looking groom was asked by a minister to repeat the following, 'I promise to be a loving, faithful and dutiful husband.' However, the nervous groom's effort was, 'I promise to be a loving, faithful and beautiful husband.' It's easily done.

But don't worry, officials get nervous, too. Couples over the years have been informed that they are to be joined in holy deadlock, with many a Scottish groom being told, 'You may now cuss the bride.'

Kate's Story

'The lengths some men will go to to avoid a simple thing like marriage. Hamish fainted at the altar. One minute there was a weak smile and a bit of sweat around his mouth, the next he was on the floor. I mean, "I do" is not exactly a speech. What a wally! He'll never live it down! To be truthful he is really quite sweet. In fact the reason I took his name was so no one else could have it.'

💜 SCOTTISH PRE-NUPTIAL AGREEMENT: WHIT'S YOURS IS MINE, AN' WHIT'S MINE IS MA AIN.

Paddy and Sarah's Story

'Did we have a quiet wedding? We certainly did. Paddy and myself were hoarse from all the shouting we did at our hen and stag nights, and in addition the official had a touch of laryngitis. Most of the guests couldn't hear the vows!'

💜 THE GOOD LORD GAVE MAN FIRE, AND HE INVENTED FIRE ENGINES. THEN HE GAVE HIM LOVE, AND HE INVENTED MARRIAGE.

Joan's Story

'Talk about exchanging rings. We nearly exchanged blows. He had clearly had a drink before the ceremony and so had his twit of a best man. He had a stupid look on his face during the service. Just wait till I get you in the limo, I thought to myself. I had a few sharp words with him in the car going to the reception, including, "All you're going to be capable of tonight is sleep!" That sort of sobered him up and I noticed at the reception he stuck to orange juice.'

Officials also should be prepared for weddings, unlike one minister who was returning to his manse located beside the church, having had a relaxing round of golf and a pleasant dram afterwards. He was getting his golf clubs out of the boot of his car, and looked up as a bridal car stopped outside the church. Five minutes later, still wearing his golfing gear under his robe, he stood solemnly at the front of the church to carry out the wedding ceremony.

Priests and ministers have been known to marry up to three couple in one day. These officials refer to such activities as 'marrythons'. But even officials can get carried away with the occasion as the following poem demonstrates.

We're aw dry wi' the drinkin' o't,
We're aw dry wi' the drinkin' o't,
The minister kissed the blushin' bride,
An' couldna preach fur thinkin' o't.

There are many versions of blessings and vows used either during the ceremony itself, or on invitation cards, wedding programmes or menus:

May God be with you and bless you,
May you see your children's children.
May you be poor in misfortune.
Rich in blessing.

May you know nothing but happiness.
May your joys be as a summer's morn,
With hearts full of love and cheer.
And may all your troubles be shadows
That fade in the sunshine of your love.

The Vows

Many couples are now into DIY vows based on their feelings and wishes for the marriage. Such vows could be:

Groom:
I promise to be a loving, dutiful husband as long as you manage to be ready on time, for once.

Or:
I promise to be a loving, dutiful husband who shares all his income, puts the toilet seat down, and cleans my golf gear myself. So long as you don't drag me round the shops of a Saturday.

Or:
I promise to be a loving, dutiful husband, only go to home matches, put no more than ten pounds on the gee-gees each week, provided you send me love and kisses in a text message every day.

Or:
I promise to be a loving, dutiful husband, who will not spend all evening on my computer, and who will take you out for a meal once

a week, and always buy you roses on our wedding anniversary.

Bride:
I promise to care for you in sickness and in health, not go over my credit limit on my Mastercard, provided you look after me, too.

Or:
I will submit and will obey, As long as you let me have my way.

Or:
I promise to be a faithful wife, remember how to put petrol in the car, and comfort you when Aberdeen lose even though my dad is a Rangers supporter.

Or:
I promise to love, honour, and not keep pulling the duvet over to my side of the bed, and not watch Coronation Street *and* EastEnders *all the time.*

Perhaps the couple may opt for more traditional vows:
> *I take you in all honour and love.*
> *In all duty and service.*
> *In all faith and tenderness.*

Or:
I promise to love, cherish and protect, in good fortune and adversity.

Whatever your chosen vows, make sure you say them to your intended, and not to the official. Look into their eyes. Fair makes your granny cry that wee bit more.

The Blessings

'The Road Ahead Blessing'
The road we travelled to reach this hour of
    happiness
Stretches behind us,
Even as the future lies ahead.
It is a long and winding road
Whose every turn will mean discovery.
With hopes, new laughter, even shared fears.
Yes, the great adventure has now started.

'The Apache Wedding Blessing'
Now you will feel no rain,
For each of you will be shelter to the other.
Now you will feel no cold,
For each of you will be warmth to the other.
Now there will be no loneliness,
For each of you will be companion to the other.
Now you are two persons,
But there are three lives before you: his life,
    her life and your life together.
Go now to your dwelling place to enter into
    your days together.

And may all your days be good and long
upon the earth.

In the spirit of the Apache Wedding Blessing there is also
the Scottish Apache Wedding Blessing:

We will still feel plenty o' rain,
For we stay in this land o' rain.
We will still feel the cauld,
Because it gets awfa cauld here at times.
But we'll be able tae have a wee cuddle,
Keep the warmth of oor love alive.
Now there will be no loneliness,
Except when he is at the match or I'm at the
bingo. [Activities optional]
Now we are two persons,
But there are many lives now: his life, her
life, oor life thegither, an' maybe some
weans.
So we are going tae oor wee 'but an' ben' to
start oor life thegether.
And may aw oor days in Scotland be braw
and lang, well, lang enough tae see
Scotland win the World Cup.

Eventually you hear the wonderful words: 'It is my privilege
and pleasure to tell you that you are now man and wife. You

may kiss the bride.' Yippee! You then go and sign the register/schedule of marriage using the required black fountain pen. Please note you are not allowed to keep this pen!

Now you are no longer just an item. You're a *legal* item.

Episode 4: 'Say Cheese, Please'

The Line-up and Photographs

> 'WAD SOME POWER THE GIFTIE GIE US, TAE SEE OORSELS AS ITHERS SEE US.'

Your wedding is unique and unrepeatable. The most important day of your life. So who is going to capture these precious memories for posterity? Is it to be old Uncle Matt with his sixties Kodak, or a posh upmarket photographer, or even the paparazzi? (You should be so lucky!)

An awkward part of any wedding is when guests arrive at the reception, then stand around for interminable hours over one drink (perhaps a dram, a bottle of beer, Buck's Fizz, wine or soft drink) trying to make polite conversation, while waiting on some slow-coach of a photographer to get on with his masterpieces, either in the hotel or at some local beauty spot.

Eventually the guests, having finally opted not to send for Red Cross parcels to quell their growing hunger pains, are joined by the principals: the bride and groom getting the red carpet welcome.

Then it is line-up time, the traditional moment when you can pass on your congratulations, smile and then kiss the best man/bridesmaid/groom/bride/whom you secretly fair fancy. Of course if it is a 'posh do' then there may be a wee mannie to shout out the guests' names.

Sometimes when you look at wedding photos you can just tell that the bride and groom are totally bathed in the glow of their affection for one another – or have had one glass of champagne too many.

Joan's Story

'My advice to anyone getting married is pay for the best photographer around. Our photos were okay, but not exactly brilliant. They will give our children something to laugh at in the years to come, assuming we do have some. Stevie Wonder could have taken better shots.'

'He's a real artist, this photographer-'

♥ MARRIAGE IS A MUTUAL RELATIONSHIP, PROVIDED
BOTH PARTIES KNOW WHEN TO BE MUTE.

Anne's Story

'On our anniversary we get out the video of the wedding and play it while drinking champagne. Your memories tend to blur as time goes by. Actually when we play it we notice small details we had both forgotten about.'

♥ 'KEEP YOUR MARRIAGE YOUNG WITH HUGS, A SQUEEZE OF THE HAND, OR AN UNEXPECTED COMPLIMENT.

'The bride and the photographer have just texted back. From the airport. They've eloped.'

Episode 5: 'Three Tiers for the Bride and Groom!'

The Wedding Cake

> GETTING MARRIED IS LIKE GOING TO STARBUCKS WITH FRIENDS. YOU ORDER A COOKIE, THEN YOU SEE WHAT THE OTHER PERSON'S GOT AND YOU WISH YOU HAD ORDERED THAT.

In ancient times the wedding cake would consist of wheat or barley, and would be broken over the bride's head as a symbol of her fertility. Gradually the tradition changed to a number of cakes placed one on top of another. The bridal pair then had to kiss over this tower, making sure they did not knock it down.

Cutting the cake is still a ritual celebration at the reception. The bride and groom make the first cut together, symbolising their shared future. The groom should place his right hand over the right hand of the bride, her left hand is placed on the top and she places the point of the knife at the centre of the bottom tier, and together they slowly cut the cake.

All the guests will be given a piece of the cake, and traditionally the bridesmaids will place theirs under their pillows (bit messy!) and dream of their own future husbands.

So what's it to be? Umpteen tiers with royal icing sides, piped icing borders, fondant on top, or your Auntie

Wilma's homemade Madeira sponge with butter-cream and her sticky icing; or it could be individual cupcakes, one for each guest. Perhaps a miniature bride and groom on the top, just so long as the image of the bride doesn't remind you of the Bride of Frankenstein.

Then there are the folks who make their own cake. It has not been unknown for the groom to make his own cake, something like turkeys voting for Christmas.

For many people the type and design of the cake may depend on the season of the year in which the wedding is taking place. For spring weddings, floral designs and delicate hues in pastel colours are a good choice. Summer weddings may have a cake incorporating chocolate-dipped strawberries. Autumn cakes may have fondant fruit such as apples and pears. In winter, sugar pine cones tinged with glistening gold make a lovely decoration.

Or how about adding a little extra frisson by having a chocolate fountain instead of the traditional cake? Rather than having your photo taken with the cake, have it taken beside warm sumptuous chocolate flowing down, with you dipping strawberries, cherries, profiteroles or marshmallows into the hot chocolate. And with the heavenly smell, your guests will be desperate to sample the pleasures of this creative fondue.

If you opt for the traditional cake, and you wish to retain a tier for any christening, then a chocolate fountain in the foyer of your reception area can be a wonderful ice-breaker.

If you go for the traditional cake then you will require a catering knife for the cutting, or as it's a Scottish wedding, perhaps a claymore.

Then there are the wedding favours to consider: sometimes five sugared almonds, representing health, wealth, happiness, fertility and long life, all wrapped in ornamental paper, then presented to the female guests during the reception.

Chocolate Fountain

Ingredients for a Scottish Wedding Cake
Lots of attraction.
Oodles of love.
A pinch of humour.
A little tolerance.
Some milk of human kindness.
Kisses and hugs.
A wee bit of hanky-panky.

Some self-forgetfulness.
A sprinkling of laughter.
A measure of consistency.
Then bake slowly, taste and enjoy!

Episode 6: 'You cannae sit them next to your Auntie Mary!'

The Meal and Seating Arrangements

> SOME AULD GABS' GOSSIP IS SO INTERESTING YOU
> ALMOST WISH YOU KNEW THE PERSON THEY WERE
> TALKING ABOUT.

'Ladies and gentlemen, please be upstanding to receive your bride and groom' heralds the normal start to the wedding breakfast: the eat, drink and be merry time.

In olden days in Scotland 'penny weddings' were common, when guests were expected to bring their own food and drink to the celebrations. Modern families would be 'black affronted' even to contemplate such an event.

Adam and Eve probably fell out about the catering arrangements. No doubt he wanted ribs and she wanted apples. And it still goes on to this day, now complicated because of individual requirements for gluten-free, vegetarian or vegan meals. At least the children present will

be happy with a mountain of chips, a burger and oodles of ketchup. Or it may be a Jewish or Muslim wedding, in which case the meal requirements must be strictly adhered to.

First question is whether guests be given a choice of meal or is it a 'take it or leave it' job? Second question: will it be a buffet (usually cheaper) or a sit down to an elegant, yummy, plated meal? Will there be an evening buffet, and of what will that comprise? Please note that if you just invite skinny, size 0, Posh Spice wannabes it could save you money; three grapes and a black coffee would just about do it.

The running buffet during the evening is primarily for those not in the 'Premier League of Invitees', commonly referred to as 'the evening guests'. For everybody else the evening buffet is an opportunity to soak up the booze.

Scottish Crab

Unfortunately weddings can provide the perfect arena for family drama. Nowadays, it is possible that the bride and groom may have 'multiple parents'. This can clearly cause potential hurt and problems, and seating arrangements have to be very carefully thought out. Old adversaries should not be seated at the same table. What is required is love, laughter and friendship, not arguments.

Step-parents, ex-husbands and ex-wives may have to be treated with kid gloves. As weddings should be joyful occasions, peace and goodwill are fundamental. A little compromise on the day is necessary, and a well-considered table plan essential. Otherwise things may get 'interesting'.

It is recommended that the tables for the meal are round. This will allow everyone at the table to participate in conversation.

Anne's Story

'Someone suggested that it would be cute to rotate our guests during the meal after every course. A number was put at every table place. Odd numbers moved on after the starter, then after the soup, then the main course, then the sweet, then the coffee. This must have been the worst idea ever. It nearly spoiled the wedding. My stepmother sat next to her ex (whom she hates with a vengeance) during the main course. I couldn't look. Talk about a nervous bride, I was petrified. When the meal was over I gave a great sigh of relief.'

♥ 'KEEP YOUR EYES OPEN BEFORE MARRIAGE, HALF SHUT AFTER MARRIAGE.

Cherie's Story

'My future in-laws were paying for the wedding, and they recommended an up-market country house which they liked. Both Billy and I went along with this, then discovered that the maximum number of guests they could accommodate for dinner was ninety, and we were inviting over a hundred and fifty. The manager persuaded us that we should have two sittings for the meal.

What a disaster that was. Billy and I were piped in twice. The top table were all given two dinners, though most just toyed with them second time around. After that everyone had to repeat their speeches. To make it worse, Billy's best man had lost his speech notes, was the worse for wear, looked glazed, zombified, and told a very naughty joke at the second sitting which he hadn't the first time around. The guests from the first sitting were a bit fed up waiting for the dance and quite a few people left early.'

♥ 'MARRIED MEN SHOULD FORGET THEIR MISTAKES. IT'S NO USE TWO PEOPLE REMEMBERING THE SAME THINGS.

Donald and Elaine's Story
'During the dessert a waitress tripped and a whole platter of crêpes suzette went over my father, and he was paying for the wedding!

However he got cleaned up and all was well. The hotel paid for him to get a new suit. He was actually quite pleased as the suit he had been wearing was quite a few years old.'

♥ THE LOVE YOU GIVE WILL DETERMINE THE LOVE YOU GET BACK.

Episode 7: It's Showtime!

The Speeches

'IF YOU WANT TO BE SEEN, STAND UP. 'IF YOU WANT TO BE HEARD, SPEAK UP. 'IF YOU WANT TO BE APPRECIATED, SIT DOWN AND SHUT UP!

The occasion at which most people find themselves called upon to make a speech is a wedding.

A good speaker at a wedding reception must know his material well, be capable of improvisation based on happenings at the wedding, know who will be at the reception, be reasonably sober, and know the fastest way out of the hall. The best speeches are well rehearsed so that you are comfortable with the material. Someone once said that a good speech is like a good shoe; it won't wear out from polishing. Just don't tell those gathered that you will not speak for long and then, having raised their hopes, be interminable and boring.

'And now just a few words —

It is much better to restrict alcohol intake to one quick quaff of champagne prior to speaking, just to calm the nerves. Legless is cringing. An embarrassingly inebriated individual attempting to tell risqué stories can spoil a whole reception.

The running order of speeches at Scottish weddings usually goes as follows: firstly the bride's father toasts the bride and groom. The bridegroom replies on behalf of himself and the bride, then toasts the bridesmaids. Then comes the best man.

The bride's father's speech is expected to be sincere but with some witty words. It should ideally express joy at this happiest of events. Sometimes the old boy may get emotional with his heartfelt, tear-jerking oratory, resulting in not a dry eye in the house. Then he may have to stop for a wee snifter of the hard stuff.

The bridegroom's speech will thank the guests for coming and also their kindness. He will thank the bride's parents and say something complimentary about the bridesmaids.

Depending on his skill as a

speaker, his discourse can be a mixture of humour and sincerity.

The best man at a wedding will know the bridegroom well, and it is expected that some friendly leg-pulling will comprise part of his speech. Some slightly naughty tales may be acceptable, but one cannot be impervious to who is present. Just remember that the parents will probably be there . . . plus old Auntie Mabel, so funny does not mean vulgar. Profanities will just upset an audience, and in no way should you refer to ex-partners on either side. Funnies should be understood by all the guests; in-jokes which only a few will recognise should be discouraged.

The best man will respond to the toast to the bridesmaids. He may also read out any cards, wedding e-cards, or congratulatory emails.

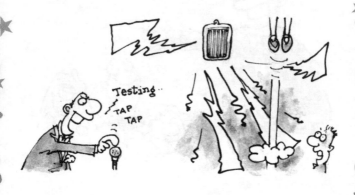

Let your speech be memorable for all the right reasons, including humour, which is always the number one crowd pleaser. Be sure to mention the bride as it is her big day. Ensure that you have been provided with a first-class microphone; weeks of preparation can be wasted if very few people actually catch what you are saying.

Some weddings are given an extra dimension by the introduction of a sweepstake. Forms are provided at each table place and guests are expected to guess the length of each speech. Afterwards, at the dance, the winner is announced and a bottle of bubbly duly handed over as the prize.

Just remember the ABCXYZ rules of speaking: 'Always Be Concise and Examine Your Zip.' And don't worry, it'll be a skoosh, especially if you remember this little poem:

> I love a finished speaker,
> I really, really do.
> I don't mean one who's polished,
> I just mean one who's through.

Note: Readers are free to use any of the material from those speeches.

Wedding of Cheryl and Alan – Father of the Bride Speech

'Ladies and gentlemen: when Alan phoned me to ask my permission to propose to Cheryl, I was somewhat taken aback. Well, it was the first reverse-charge call I had had for quite a while. Actually, when he asked for Cheryl's hand in marriage I replied that it was fine as long as it was the hand that used to be continually in my pocket.

'As you know, the man in a marriage must be the boss. So, if you want any advice on matrimony, Alan, then come and see me after seven-thirty on a Monday night. The wife's out then.

'I actually thought when I proposed to my wife Pat that it was to marry me, but evidently I was merely challenging her to a series of debates. We recently celebrated our thirty-fifth wedding anniversary. We had a two-minute silence! Yes, marriage is bliss, but then again so is ignorance. However, I must say that in all our married years we have never once considered divorce. Murder, yes, but never divorce.

'Did you know that the word wedding derives from "wedd", a pledge to marry. Apparently long ago the groom, with the help of his best warrior friend, now called the best man, would kidnap the woman and fight off other men who wanted her. I am so glad that things are much more civilised and I can willingly give Cheryl away with my blessing on this marriage. I must say that I could not have given her away to a better man than Alan. It is said that a good husband makes a good wife, and a good wife makes a good husband. But it is up to the two of you to make a good marriage.

'Cheryl and Alan have been living together for almost two years, but I always say that living together without getting married is like being punished for a crime you didn't commit!

'I know that Cheryl and Alan originally met through this mysterious internet, which I do not fully understand. Nowadays there are many different ways to meet your future spouse. A man was on the Glasgow to Edinburgh train when he became aware that the lady opposite was staring at him. She said to him, "Do you know, you look just like my third husband." He replied, "Oh, you have been married three times, then?" "No," she said, "just twice."

'Now let me give a word of warning to Alan. Cheryl will tell you, but you probably know this already, that she has nothing to wear. But I bet her wardrobes are packed so tightly that there are moths in there that haven't learned to fly yet.

'Now it is time for the toast. I am tempted to make the toast, "To marriage, the last decision a man is allowed to make", but instead, ladies and gentlemen, please charge your glasses and be upstanding for the real toast, "The Bride and Groom".'

Wedding of Cheryl and Alan – Bridegroom's Speech

'Ladies and gentlemen: on behalf of my wife and myself, I would like to thank you all for coming along today. I was actually given very good advice a year ago that I should marry my lovely

Cheryl. The advice came from Cheryl!

'I would also like to thank the people who made Cheryl, namely her mum and dad. I may well take her dad's advice at seven-thirty on a Monday night. Perhaps he can throw in a beer.

'Did you know that during the wedding ceremony the bride always stands on the left of the groom? This is so that his sword arm is free and he can fend off attackers. Luckily I have not been required to resort to anything like this today ... so far. It is also the custom that the groom holds on to the bride with his left hand. So the relatives and guests of Cheryl now know why you sat on the left-hand side seats during the ceremony today. You never know, this information may be valuable to you one day if you're on *Who Wants to be a Millionaire*.

'Today is a really special day for me as I have now married the woman I love, which makes me the luckiest man in the whole of Scotland. Cheryl today has metamorphosed from a Miss to a Mrs, and I'm the fortunate mister.

'Also, on behalf of my wife and myself I wish to thank you for your lovely gifts. Everyone has been extremely kind to us. Your generosity has been overwhelming.

'This in fact is the happiest day of my life, and I must thank my new wife for pointing that out to me. When we first met, as you have just heard, it was on the internet. I never ever thought that it would lead to me standing here today thanking my new father-in-law for proposing the health of the bride and groom.

'The first time I actually saw Cheryl I thought she was stunning. So I said, "You're gorgeous." And she replied, "Drop dead!" Since then we have progressed somewhat but I can honestly say today, Cheryl, you are "drop-dead gorgeous".

'I now wish to present my new wife with a spirtle. For those of you who do not know about this tradition, many Scots give their wives wooden spoons, called spirtles, in order that she can stir his porridge of a morning. Now Cheryl has no excuse for not making breakfast.

'Cheryl has been most fortunate with her choice of bridesmaids today. I am sure you will agree they have done us proud. Their beauty and presence have contributed significantly to our day.

'And so, in the time-honoured way, ladies and gentlemen, I give you the toast of "The Bridesmaids".'

Wedding of Cheryl and Alan – Best Man's Speech

'Ladies and gentlemen: Cheryl has always liked skinny men and the reason she selected Alan is that he looks like the gable end of a ten-pound note. In fact when he goes to the park the ducks throw him bread, and he never ever walks over cattle grids.

'In all sincerity I have got to say that Alan is a lucky man. You've got Cheryl. She's beautiful, intelligent, funny, warm and loving.

'Cheryl, you've got Alan!

'And now, ladies and gentlemen, the management of this esteemed establishment have asked me to make an announcement. For reasons of your own personal safety, at the end of this speech you should refrain from getting on to tables and chairs for my standing ovation.

'I feel like the young Arab sheikh who inherited his father's harem. I know what to do but am uncertain where to start. However, today is a very special day. On this day in June 1314, Scotland won the Battle of Bannockburn. On this day in 1790 Rabbie Burns wrote his poem Tam O'Shanter. On this day our sweethearts, Cheryl and Alan, were married. And on this day you heard the best best man's speech you will

ever hear from me, old Bighead himself! But as Henry the Eighth said to each of his wives, "I shall not keep you too long."

'We are here to celebrate the marriage of two clever people. Alan is good at maths while Cheryl has an aptitude for languages. Last time she was in Italy she picked up a little Italian. I just hope that on their honeymoon in Sorrento she doesn't run into him.

'But I am sure the future will bring not just travelling but many little additions to your marriage. May I say congratulations on the termination of your isolation, and may I express an appreciation of your determination to end the desperation and frustration which caused you so much consternation in giving you the inspiration to make a combination to hopefully bring accumulations to the population!

'Today without some wonderful people this wedding reception would not have been the same. So please fill your glasses and be upstanding for the toast. Ladies and gentlemen I give you ... the bar staff!

'Just kidding! Please sit down until I finish my speech.

'As a bachelor myself I know little of marriage. Though someone did tell me that the most dangerous year in married life is the first. Then follows the second, the third, the fourth, fifth...

'As you are aware Alan is no spring-chicken. In fact he had got to the stage when he thought that "getting a little action" merely indicated his prune juice was working. He had also got to the stage where his back went out more often than he did. Now Cheryl will know what it's like to have old age creeping up on her.

'But Alan is a fine specimen who always keeps himself in shape; at home he even has his own parallel bars; one for whisky and one for brandy.

'You may know that I am someone who will drink to anything, so, ladies and gentlemen, on behalf of the bridesmaids I'd be most happy if you would give me an excuse to raise my glass by joining me in a toast to the happiness of everyone here.'

Wedding of Chloe and John – Father of the Bride Speech

'Distinguished guests: on behalf of my bank manager and myself, it gives me great pleasure on this special occasion to wish every happiness to Chloe and John in their married life together.

'I started today with two daughters and a son and have ended the day with two daughters and two sons. It is indeed an honour to welcome John into our family. Both my wife and myself are delighted that Chloe has now got such an excellent fellow for her husband. I truly feel they were made for each other. Also the two families have met on a number of occasions and got on famously.

'Of course there will be problems and no doubt quarrels ahead. When my wife and I got married over thirty years ago, I thought she was an angel. Actually I still do. The reason for this is that she is usually flying around here and there, she's never got anything to wear, and is always harping on about something.

'You will learn, Chloe and John, that

marriage teaches you loyalty, forbearance, self-restraint and a lot of other qualities you wouldn't have required had you stayed single.

'At least today's proceedings have gone ahead as planned. I heard recently of a bride in Gourock who was jilted at the altar. She was so distraught that she stowed away on a ship to America. After a week she was caught and brought before the captain. She told him, "Captain, your first officer has been kind to me, he's looked after me, fed me, and you could say, he's taken advantage of me." "You can say that again," said the captain. "This is the Gourock to Dunoon ferry."

'You may well know that Chloe and John have been going out with each other for nearly seven years. I thought today was never going to happen. But now that it has I nearly got the organist to change his music from the *Wedding March* to the *Hallelujah Chorus*!

'You know, it used to be in Scotland that the wedding ceremony would merely be the swearing of an oath on a Bible held over a running stream. In fact this is the way Rabbie Burns married his Highland Mary. Today's ceremony was somewhat different, and if I may say so, just wonderful. Everything went ever so well. An Oscar-winning performance for the two in the starring roles. Two people terribly in love and deliriously happy. And now I have lost my 'Little Princess' to a younger man.

'Finally I wish to thank you all for coming. It would not have been the same without you. It would have been cheaper!

'So, as a non-practising teetotaller, I would ask you to charge your glasses, and stand with me for the toast of "The Bride and Groom".'

Wedding of Chloe and John – Bridegroom's Speech

'Ladies and gentlemen: you are here to witness a unique event. The very first time, and probably the very last time, that my wife is going to let me speak on behalf of us both.

'So on behalf of my wife and myself let me thank you for coming to our wedding today. I just love a distinguished, intelligent, good-looking audience. Thank you for making this day special and I wish to thank you sincerely for all your wonderful, thoughtful presents.

'It is said that marriage is when a man and a woman become one: the trouble starts when they try to decide which one. However, I am confident we will really always be together, as one.

'You may be aware that Chloe and I actually met at a wedding reception. Therefore I thought it appropriate that I shock you today and break into song.

> A fine wee lass, a bonnie wee lass, is bonnie
>   wee Chloe McColl,
> I gave her my mother's engagement ring and
>   a bonnie wee tartan shawl.
> I met her at a waddin' in the Co-operative
>   hall.
> I was the best man and she was the belle of
>   the ball.

'Today, my Chloe is certainly the belle of the ball. By profession she is a trolley-dolly with British Airways – you could no doubt tell that by the way she walked down the aisle.

'I set out to find the perfect woman. One who didn't smoke, didn't drink, didn't take drugs and wasn't interested in other men. Well, I eventually found one. She's our four-year-old flower-girl, Daisy!

'I must say that the first part of our marriage was blissfully happy, then, in the car coming from the ceremony . . .

'I heard of a minister who was asked to

perform a short wedding ceremony at the end of a Sunday morning service. When the service finished he planned to ask the couple to come forward from their seats within the congregation, but for the life of him he couldn't remember their names. So he just announced, "Would those wanting to get married please come to the front." Immediately, six single ladies, five widows, four widowers and three single men stepped to the front. So you see, marriage is an institution that many people wish to join.

'I am so pleased that both Chloe's father and mother get on so well with my own parents. It has made the whole thing so much easier for my new wife and myself. Thank you Sandy and Rose for your wonderful hospitality today, and for allowing me to marry your beautiful daughter.

'I believe looking around that we have all had a good time. But all good things must come to an end. With that in mind I must tell you that my best man will shortly speak.

'It is my duty, as you know, to say some words of appreciation to the three bridesmaids today. You have been delightful, and I know Thom, my best man, has been eyeing you up all day.

'There are three reasons for drinking. One is when you are thirsty. The second is to prevent thirst. The third is to make a toast. Please now be upstanding with a brimming glass in your hand to drink the health of our lovely bridesmaids, Lynne, Jill and Mary. Ladies and gentlemen, "The Bridesmaids".'

Wedding of Chloe and John – Best Man's Speech

'Ladies and gentlemen: for those of you who are unaware, I must tell you I'm not married myself. I just look this way because I have been ill.

'So what do I say about John? I first met him at university. Since that time I've watched him grow from a cheeky, young, immature drunk to a cheeky, old, immature drunk. Just kidding as I know he hardly touches the stuff … now!

'I have known John from way back when he had hair. You can actually judge a man by his baldness. If he is bald at the front, he is a great thinker. If he is bald at the back, he is a great lover. John is bald at the front and the back and just thinks he is a great lover. Communication of course is the key to love and sex. I recently heard of a bride who gave up sex for Lent but her husband didn't find out till Christmas.

'As you will know, John is a GP but he's still learning the doctoring business. For instance he thinks that a "house call" means some sort of bingo ritual. Actually my grandfather didn't believe in doctors. He always treated himself from an old book of remedies. Unfortunately he died of a printer's error.

'Today John and Chloe have achieved lasting fame with everyone here. So what is fame? Fame is like being invited to Number 10 Downing Street to talk to the prime minister. No, that's not fame. Fame is when you are talking to the prime minister, the phone goes and he ignores it. No, that's not fame either. Fame is when you are talking to the prime minister and the phone goes, he answers it, holds it out to you and says, "It's Chloe for you, John."

'I would also like to congratulate Chloe's parents on the way they restrained themselves today. After all, it can't be easy to see your daughter marrying someone like my pal John!

'I always regard myself as a person who can very quickly sum up other people. When I first met Chloe my immediate impression was of someone who was shrewd, discerning, clever and thoughtful. But she soon proved me wrong by agreeing to marry John.

'Actually John nearly didn't make today's wedding. He had to have a minor sports operation. It was to get the TV remote removed from his hand as he was watching the rugby. In fact John and Chloe both live in a totally hi-tech world. With the number of daily texts they have sent each other over the last year, I was surprised today they didn't put their rings on their texting thumbs.

'I was talking to one of the flower girls at the start of the reception, and I asked her, "Will you get married one day?"

'"Yes," she said, "I'm going to marry the wee boy next door."

'I said, "Is he a nice wee boy, then?"

'She replied, "Not really, but my daddy

says I'm not allowed to cross the road."

'Remember folks, there are seven deadly sins... enough for one each day! And with the generous open bar tonight no doubt some of you here will be indulging in some of these sins pretty soon. Of course John will not now drink anything stronger than pop. Mind you, I know his pop will drink anything. Which brings me to our lovely bridesmaids and flower girls. They have looked after Chloe so well and radiated smiles and sunshine all day.

'So on their behalf and mine, let me thank you all for making this day so special.

'Thank you.'

Wedding of Flo and Martin – Father of the Bride Speech

'Ladies and gentlemen: I'd like to thank you all for coming, especially those of you who knew I'd be saying a few words but turned up anyway. I believe that to make a successful speech one should follow the formula of the three Gs. Be gracious, grateful and then get off!

'I stand here as a proud father and it is with great pleasure that I am able to wish Flo and Martin every happiness at the start of their married life together. You know, the marriage of a daughter is a passage in any father's life and I am glad it has all gone off swimmingly today.

'Well, the "happy pair" certainly did not keep us long in suspense once they decided to be wed. They are quite right. If they want a golden wedding they need to get on with it.

'I thought that today's ceremony was most moving. Everyone looked so smart, the church was wonderfully decorated and the words selected for both the vows and hymns were just right.

'Today was an opportunity for both sets of family and friends to meet, get to know each other and, I trust, get on with each other.

'No doubt the happy pair will have their ups and downs along life's way. But your marriage will be what you make of it. The bonds of matrimony are not worth much if the interest is not kept up. Knowing you two, I have every confidence that this marriage will be a long-lasting success.

'I cannot be too critical of Flo. She has been a wonderful daughter. I mean, spending money is her only extravagance. Probably takes after her mother. Early on in my own marriage I made a dreadful mistake and opened a joint current account with my darling wife, which unfortunately allows her to beat me to the draw.

'Next to my wife, my only child Flo is my number one prized asset, so you take good care of her, Martin. I wish that your love for each other be modern enough to survive these times, yet old fashioned enough to last for ever.

'Martin, he is a great chap with his many business interests, although I am a bit fed up losing to him at golf. I don't believe his handicap of fifteen. He's a bit of a bandit, you know. Now that he has the responsibilities of marriage upon him I am hoping this will allow me to occasionally get the better of him on the course.

'Ladies and gentlemen, we wish the happy pair well on their travels, not just on honeymoon but throughout life, and with that I would ask you to please charge your glasses and rise to drink a toast to the happy couple, Martin and Flo.'

Wedding of Flo and Martin – Bridegroom's Speech

'Ladies and gentlemen: first of all let me thank my father-in-law for his kind words and advice. Then let me thank you all for coming and making this a day Flo and I will never forget.

'Some people say that marriage is like the lottery. If that is so I must have had all my numbers up because I have won the top prize today. Isn't Flo just superb? Now she will be called Mrs MacIntyre, and she's my Mrs MacIntyre. It is just great to have a better half, a help-mate, and such a lovely spouse.

'So, on behalf of Mrs MacIntyre and myself, thank you all for coming today to join with us on our special day. Thank you all for your lovely presents. You have been most kind.

'A really special thanks must also go to our parents for their generous assistance in today's proceedings.

'I also wish to thank my lovely bride for marrying me. She has made me the happiest man in the world today. Didn't she just look wonderful as she came down the aisle? And did you notice that Flo shed a little tear during the vows, hopefully for the right reasons. So I can now say that I have ... got myself a cryin', talkin', sleepin', walkin', livin' doll! And I would further like to praise her in her choice of groom! Also her choice of bridesmaids. Aren't they just lovely and haven't they done us proud today?

'I want to thank my mother and father and Flo's mum and dad for being ideal parents. I only hope that Flo and myself make as good a job of our married lives together as you have.

'You know, everybody has been reminding me of our wedding today. Only this morning I saw the motorist behind me in my mirror, sticking up his finger to remind me that this was my big day. So I just held up two of my fingers to tell him the wedding was at two o'clock!

'Flo may be a petite lady, but I have always said it is better to have loved a short girl than never to have loved at all.

'It is now my pleasure to especially thank the ladies in both our lives, namely our mums, and to present to them an appreciation of our love, namely these bouquets.

'It is almost time for my best man, Paul, to speak. If you are looking for quality and wit in a speech he's your man. In fact people have been looking for quality and wit in his speeches for years.

'Before that experience I must say a big sincere thank you to our lovely bridesmaids. They have carried out their duties admirably. Ladies and gentlemen, I invite you to join with me and be upstanding for the toast of "The Bridesmaids".'

Wedding of Flo and Martin – Best Man's Speech

'Ladies and gentlemen: I have the honour today

of replying on behalf of the bridesmaids. Don't they just look wonderful in their pink dresses? They'll be on eBay next week, of course.

'Tonight I am not going to bore you with stories about the battle of the sexes, equality in marriage, feminine wiles, male chauvinism and such malarkey. No, no, no. I will just welcome you here today, and ask, did you turn off the lights and gas before you came out?

'I am honoured to be Martin's best man, though it was touch and go whether or not the prison governor gave him a twenty-four-hour parole pass.

'Looking around here tonight, I doubt if there has been such a prestigious concentration of intelligentsia, academia and colossi present since the last time Martin dined alone. But I also have to tell you that Martin was a slow starter in life. He was different from all the other six-year-old boys in his class; he was twelve. In fact when his grandmother asked him what he thought he would be when he left school, he replied, "About thirty."

'Martin knows how to treat a lady properly. On their very first date he took Flo for a meal in his car to a classy, chic little open-air bistro. I believe it's called a McDonald's Drive-In.

'Weddings are great places to meet up with your relatives, aren't they? Much better than meeting up at funerals when someone always says, "Too bad we can't do this more often."

'And it is essential, Martin, you never upset your new wife. As the old Chinese saying goes, "Never argue with spouse who pack your parachute."

'As you are probably aware, both Martin and Flo are churchgoers. So my wedding present to them has been in the shape of two embroidered texts from the Good Book. They are to hang over their bed. On Flo's side of the bed the text is "I need thee every hour." On Martin's side it's "Lord, give me strength."

'Being such a beautiful woman, some people are surprised that Flo married Martin. She has in her time been pursued by many a potential suitor. Actually Flo used a unique way to select Martin. It goes like this. Eenie, meenie, miney, mo! To be fair Martin was and is by far the best of the bunch.

'Martin and Flo have been planning their exotic honeymoon somewhere romantic and quiet. Mind you, personally I would not have chosen Cumbernauld.

'On behalf of the bridesmaids and myself

can I sincerely say we have all enjoyed this lovely wedding. The day has been just perfect.

'Finally I would say to Martin and Flo: here's to love, laughter and happily ever after.

'Thank you.'

Episode 8: 'Ur Ye Dancin'?'

The Jiggin' and Drink

> 'A REAL GUID BAND IS A MUST TAE TRIP THE LIGHT
> FANTASTIC. THE ONLY THING YOU CAN DO ON A
> SHOESTRING IS TRIP.'

Now it's time for the happy couple, watched closely by their relatives and friends, both old and new, to take to the dance floor for a wee twirl, or even a well-choreographed first dance as man and wife, while having an anticipatory feel of each other's bottom. You may start off to 'Unchained Melody'. Then, after thirty seconds get the DJ to switch to 'Rockin' All Over the World!' Wow! That livens up the proceedings. The chief bridesmaid and best man will quickly take the floor, followed by the couple's parents, the groom's father dancing with the bride's mother, and the groom's mother dancing with the bride's father. Then the entire company will hopefully join in.

Is it going to be a ceilidh, a disco or a ten-piece band?

Will it be a slow shimmy mixed with a bit of rock? Will it be a matter of dancing the night away under a canvas roof? Will they all be giving it laldy? But surely, as it is a Scottish wedding, it will predominately feature Scottish country dancing? After all, *reel* men love to dance and many a Scot has learned to dance standing outside a communal cludgie. Some even may have learned to limbo dance trying to get into pay-toilets.

Just watch, though, as Scottish country dancing is quite energetic, and comprises the art of getting your feet out of the way faster than the next person can step on them. One of the most popular dances is 'Mhairi's Wedding', the words of which go as follows:

> Step we gaily, on we go,
> Heel for heel and toe for toe,
> Arm in arm and row and row,

All for Mhairi's wedding.
Plenty herring, plenty meal,
Plenty peat to fill her creel,
Plenty bonnie bairns as weel
That's the toast for Mhairi.

heel for heel
and toe for toe -

The 'creel' mentioned is a large basket, and in the song it was filled with peat. Sometimes the Highland custom of 'creeling' took place at weddings. This involved filling the creel with stones and tying it to the groom's back. He then had to carry it around the village unless his wife agreed to kiss him.

Some people, and you see many at weddings, will dance a slow foxtrot no matter what the band is playing. However, one of the wonderful things about disco style dancing is that nobody knows when you make a mistake, not even you.

Then there's the 'Birdie Song', 'YMCA', the 'Conga'

and 'Dancing Queen'. Everybody will surely be up and getting into the groove for that lot. You might also want to consider throwing in a limbo-dancing contest.

Lisa's Story

'We were in the middle of our wedding at Crieff Hydro when the fire alarm went off. The dance was going full swing in the wedding-reception area downstairs at that point, so we all trooped up the stairs, including my old grannies, and out of the Hydro to be met by two fire engines. I ended up sitting on top of a fire engine in my wedding dress surrounded by grinning firemen, having my photo taken.'

💜 NOBODY CARES HOW BAD YOUR ENGLISH IS AS LONG AS YOUR SCOTCH IS GOOD.

Fraser and Gina's Wedding

'We had what I call a fairytale wedding. By the end of it he had had so much to drink he was well and truly away with the fairies.'

💜 THEY SAY THAT BRUNETTES HAVE A SWEETER DISPOSITION THAN BLONDES AND REDHEADS. SOME WIVES HAVE IN THEIR TIME BEEN ALL THREE AND THEIR HUSBANDS COULDN'T SEE ANY DIFFERENCE.

James and Wendy's Story

'I remember looking at the heaving dance floor and there was James's Uncle Jimmy trying to stand, never mind dance. He was absolutely blotto but insisted, as drunks do, that he had to dance at his nephew's wedding. Within thirty seconds he was on the floor with poor Auntie Mamie plus a few of the guests, all of them not in a great state themselves, trying to get him up. Eventually he was deposited in a chair by the band, where he snored loudly for the rest of the proceedings.'

'THE TROUBLE WITH ME,' SAID THE HUSBAND, 'IS THAT I'M A PERFECTIONIST AND YOU'RE NOT.' REPLIED HIS WIFE, 'THAT'S WHY YOU MARRIED ME AND I MARRIED YOU.'

I mid it die way

Archie's Story

'We had a karaoke contest. I had previously pre-selected a couple of our guests to participate. They all had to sing songs featuring love. Then my father, somewhat the worse for drink, insisted he wanted to sing. Sing? He could hardy stand! It must be the worst rendition of "My Way" ever. My mother was mortified but the judges of the contest, two of my uncles, decided to make him the winner. Good idea as he was paying for the whole thing.'

MUSIC BRINGS SOME COUPLES TOGETHER.
LOVE KEEPS THEM TOGETHER.

Then there's the hard stuff. It is supposed to be bad for you, but you wouldn't know that at most Scottish weddings. After a few wee swallies of lovely bubbly the vowels tend to get somewhat slurred, the volume of noise rises and the singing increases, plus the smile on the bar manager's face becomes wider with each ringing shout of *slainte*!

It is bad for us and it certainly isn't a stimulant, but we enjoy it. It used to be that alcohol and nicotine went hand in hand, but now all the puffers present will have to go and stand out in the cold for a bit. Might just sober some of them up.

Some folks seem to quaff away all night at their hauf and haufs, and to all intents and purposes you would never know they had had a skinful. But for others, well, a couple of mouthfuls of drinky-poos and they are away smashed. That's when it can get interesting. You not only have old Uncle Wullie up giving it bell-tinkle for a karaoke number, but with the liquid libation liberally lapping livers, you can have wives and ex-husbands swapping interesting opinions! Furthermore, occasionally you get someone drunk enough to try it on with someone else's missus who is equally inebriated and compliant.

Chapter Nine:
Elixir of Love

The Honeymoon

If you want to prepare a dish for bedtime, try champagne.

It's almost that time of the wedding reception when the couple have stood as much as they can, so the bride heaves her bouquet over her head, with all the dexterity of a Scottish prop forward, into the hopeful scrum assembled behind. Then they take their leave to the sounds of 'For They Are Jolly Good Fellows' and 'Auld Lang Syne'. The

bride's parents stand and wave goodbye, whilst duly murmuring, 'Ah hope he taks good care o' oor wee lassie.'

Hot blood is coursing through the happy couple's veins so off they set in their car, which is dressed with balloons, 'Just Married' toilet paper, and trailing old shoes, to go to the bridal suite in a luxury hotel or a B&B in Pitlochry.

In the Middle East four thousand years ago, the practice was that the bride's father would supply his new son-in-law with all the mead he could drink. Mead is a honey beer, and because their calendar was lunar based, this period became known as the honey month, hence honeymoon.

After the marriage comes the nuptials, the dream honeymoon and the primal need for legalised rumpy pumpy. Where will all this activity take place? Will it be three weeks in Barbados, two weeks in Kuala Lumpur, a week in Ibiza, or a few days in Troon? If they have been smart they will have shopped around in advance and got a good honeymoon deal. Champagne, flowers, room upgrade and free first-night dinner.

The advice to men for honeymoons usually goes something like this:

> Easy oan the throttle,
> Steady wi' the gears.
> Roll her o'er gently
> An' she'll last fur years an' years.

Advice to women can be:

> Tak heed frae those who ken,
> And tie yer nightie tae yer toes,
> Close yer eyes and hold yer nose,
> Then you'll see just how it goes.

While on honeymoon the groom's pyjamas are traditionally kept under a pillow in case there is a fire. The bride should come into the hotel bedroom all coy and cute in her new nightie, hair falling softy around perfumed shoulders, and with only a bedside light on, looking the epitome of feminine desire.

Give it a few months and she will flop into bed with the curlers on, face cream from ear to ear, and a goonie her granny used to wear. And if the doorbell goes she will say, 'You go. I can't let the postman see me like this!'

On honeymoon the couple will no doubt lie back and analyse the Big Day, and recall the various goings on of their guests. Then they can analyse their pressies. If they had a wedding list, who bought which item.

Honeymoon of Craig and Fiona

'Our honeymoon was in Sicily. The first day I lost my wedding ring. The water was distinctly chilly, my fat fingers retreated and the ring slid off. I spent a good hour diving in the surf before bravely returning to my new wife on the beach. She was astonished I'd been swimming so long but somewhat nonplussed at my loss. Anyway, the most important thing is that I have her.'

♥ A HONEYMOON IS A SHORT PERIOD OF MATING BETWEEN DATING AND DEBATING.

Honeymoon of Tom and Joan

'After the wedding we set off in a cab to spend the night at a hotel. Would you believe it but the cabbie couldn't find it, and at two in the morning we returned to Joan's mother's place. All the beds were already occupied so we spent the night on a couple of sofas.'

♥ AFTER THE HONEYMOON I FELT LIKE A NEW MAN. UNFORTUNATELY SHE SAID SHE FELT LIKE ONE, TOO.

Honeymoon of Alistair and Claire

'We spent a long time planning our honeymoon. We just love climbing the Scottish hills so we thought we would really push the boat out and have an extravagant affair hiking in some South American mountains. We took along with us a local guide. Unfortunately, the weather closed in on us in no uncertain manner. There were massive storms and lightning strikes. The guide, who normally slept in his own tent nearby, insisted in sleeping in our tent one night because he was terrified.'

THE FOOD OF LOVE FOR THE HONEYMOON IS ALWAYS THE SAME, 'HONEYMOON SALAD' ... LETTUCE ALONE!

Chapter Ten: Marriage

The Final Frontier

Marriage is a relationship in which one person is always right, and the other is the husband.

Returning from honeymoon, it is customary to carry the bride over the threshold, while sweetly whispering in her ear, 'Ah thought you went tae Weight-Watchers, ma wee pet?' The reply from new brides can only be guessed at. This ancient ritual thus ensures the bride is protected from any evil spirits lurking at ground level and keeps slimming clubs in business.

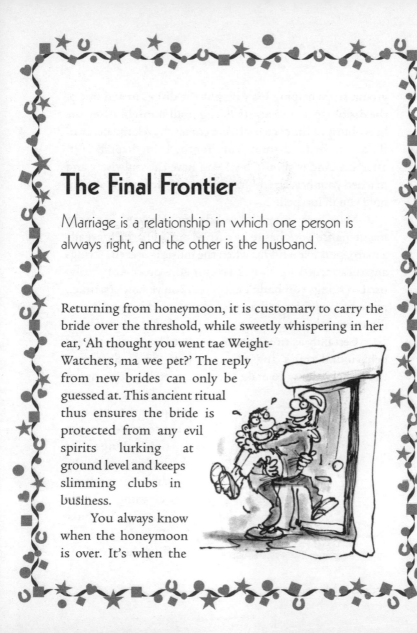

You always know when the honeymoon is over. It's when the

groom stops helping his wife put the dishes in and out of the dishwasher, and starts doing it all himself. After the hurly-burly of the car's back seat comes the relative peace of the queen sized bed, for it's time for the 'living-happily-ever-after' bit. And it should be if you have chosen wisely and married your best friend. Yes, that old black magic should hold you in its spell.

Marriages may be made in Heaven but the maintenance work has to be carried out on Earth, for really a marriage is like a fiddle; when the music is over the strings are still attached. Really it is a continuous process of getting used to things you hadn't expected. You've now got much more to worry about than just global warming and ozone depletion. At least marriage gets people to bed at a decent hour.

Certainly as time goes by you both learn each other's behavioural traits and idiosyncrasies. Some Scotsmen think that helping to make the bed is merely getting out of

it. A husband may propose that his wife concentrate on the trivial things like looking after the house, cooking, cleaning, and paying the bills. The self-appointed 'high-heid-yin' is then left to worry about big issues like football, rugby and politics. And if your man is not too keen to help with the cleaning just put the duster over the TV remote. That may get him switched on, for division of labour is a good idea. Marriage is in some ways a series of negotiations to find out the secret formula that will work out best for the couple concerned.

Just never trust a man who says he's the boss at home. He probably lies about other things, too. When such a man says he gets his breakfast in bed it is usually in hospital.

And as for the occasional little problems that have to be 'talked through', most men would rather scrub the house clean when the Scottish Cup final is on television, than discuss anything emotional.

When a courting couple kiss, they get so close they cannot see anything wrong with each other because love brings you joy and ecstasy. When a married couple kiss, they have got so close they know what's wrong with each other. For people do change after marriage, and as one exasperated wife was heard to say, 'You don't really know a man until he's tasted his own wedding cake.' A married man was also quoted as reminding his wife that she had taken him for better or for worse. To which she replied, 'Aye, but you are worse than I took you for!' It is therefore essential to keep the romance alive by reminding your spouse that he or she is still worth the time and effort that you devoted way back in the days of your courting.

Consideration and love go hand in hand. It might just be putting the toilet seat back down or remembering to record her favourite TV programme.

The truth is that no Scottish male can consider himself truly married until he understands his wife's every look, together with the words she is not saying.

Some people believe that the Scottish Enlightenment deals with that time when the Scots led the world into the modern era. They are wrong. The Scottish enlightenment happens when two Scots marry and become only too aware of the other's true characteristics and habits. Sometimes a Scottish marriage can resemble the history of Scotland: tragic ironies, lost opportunities, battles won and lost, but oh, such glorious memories!

Marriage of Peter and Cecile

'I came into the bedroom. Everything was in disarray. All the drawers were scattered every-where. I went to a neighbour and phoned the police as I didn't want to linger in case the burglar was still in the house. The police arrived within half an hour and were taking a statement from me when my husband walked in. We hadn't been burgled. He'd been looking for a clean shirt.'

♥ IF YOU THINK WOMEN ARE THE WEAKER SEX, TRY PULLING THE DUVET BACK TO YOUR SIDE.

Marriage of John and Jennifer

'I was in hospital for four days. When I came home I didn't really need to light the gas on the cooker. I could have lit the grease.'

 A SUCCESSFUL MARRIAGE DEMANDS A DIVORCE; A DIVORCE FROM YOUR OWN SELF-INTEREST.

Marriage of James and Anne

'I am a busy headmistress and for a while my husband was unemployed. During that time he agreed to do all the housework. One weekend I complained to him that I could write my name on the dust on the top of the television. He replied that that was education for you.'

 GEORGE WASHINGTON COULD NEVER TELL A LIE. WIVES CAN. AS SOON AS THEY HEAR IT!

Marriage of Dave and Margaret

'The only reason I got irritable with him was that he was so irritating. I remember one argument. He told me he was an idiot to marry me, and I just told him that I was in love and didn't notice. At one stage we were even all set to part, then we thought, who is going to have the cats? So, we just stayed together. Actually it's worked out well. In fact we are more in love than ever. The secret is to be tolerant, patient, hard-working, flexible and creative in your marriage.'

♥ SOMEONE WHO DOESN'T KNOW THAT A WIFE'S WORK IS NEVER DONE JUST ISN'T LISTENING.

Marriage of Stan and Isa

'A neighbour, who had been merrit roon aboot the same time as masel, commented that efter a while the magic jist isnae there in a marriage.

"Ur you kiddin'," ah said. "That wan o' mine can still produce the magic. Every Friday night he disappears sober and comes back half-cut."'

♥ A HAPPILY MARRIED MAN MUST ALWAYS HAVE THE LAST WORDS IN ANY ARGUMENT OR DISCUSSION. THE WORDS ARE, 'YES, DEAR' AND 'ANYTHING YOU SAY, DEAR.'

Marriage of Ian and Patricia

'The marriage is great but the biggest thrill of the last six months was running into my hubby's ex-girlfriend. She was about three sizes bigger than me. Oh, joy!'

♥ 'ROMANCE BRINGS PEOPLE TOGETHER, BUT LOVE KEEPS THEM TOGETHER.

Chapter Eleven: 'Och, prams are just last year's fun on wheels!'

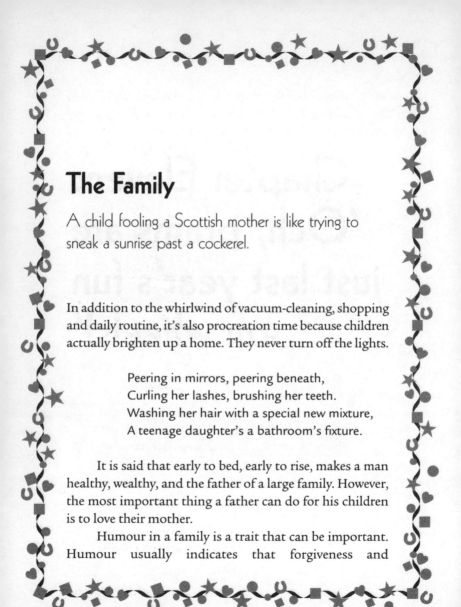

The Family

A child fooling a Scottish mother is like trying to sneak a sunrise past a cockerel.

In addition to the whirlwind of vacuum-cleaning, shopping and daily routine, it's also procreation time because children actually brighten up a home. They never turn off the lights.

> Peering in mirrors, peering beneath,
> Curling her lashes, brushing her teeth.
> Washing her hair with a special new mixture,
> A teenage daughter's a bathroom's fixture.

It is said that early to bed, early to rise, makes a man healthy, wealthy, and the father of a large family. However, the most important thing a father can do for his children is to love their mother.

Humour in a family is a trait that can be important. Humour usually indicates that forgiveness and compromise are easily found within the relationship. Each family is unique, with no one set of rules applying to all families. But a happy marriage and therefore a happy family are the foundations of a happy society.

Marriage of Billy and Dorothy

'We struggled for years to have a family. It was false hope after false hope, then we got depressed. Eventually we called our trying the "Rhythm and Blues" method. We used the rhythm method and when it didn't work we got the blues! Eventually it did and now we have wee Charlie. No more blues except when we are up during the night changing him and giving him his bottle.'

♥ 'NEWLYWEDS BECOME OLDYWEDS, AND OLDYWEDS ARE WHY LOVE AND FAMILY WORK.

Marriage of Duncan and Jeannie

'I just told him it was time for him to have a vasectomy – after all, we had four kids. He wisnae keen an' said, "Why don't you have yer fallopian tubes tied?" So ah just said, "Och, away you an' get knotted. Nae vasectomy, nae hanky-panky." Needless tae say he went an' goat wan.'

♥ THE VALUE OF MARRIAGE IS NOT THAT ADULTS PRODUCE CHILDREN BUT THAT CHILDREN PRODUCE ADULTS.

Marriage of Kevin and Kate

'I was probably about four months pregnant and it was just beginning to show, when I met up with an old friend. She had put on some weight and remarked that it was her love of beer that had done it to her. I replied, "Actually in a funny sort of way it was alcohol that did this to me too."'

♥ THE BEAUTY OF MIDDLE AGE IS THAT YOU'RE OLD ENOUGH TO KNOW BETTER BUT YOUNG ENOUGH TO GO ON DOING IT!

Chapter Twelve: 'How can you expect me to remember when you never look a day older?'

The Anniversaries

Marriage is the alliance of two people, one of whom never remembers birthdays and anniversaries, and the other who never forgets them.

It is said that the only way to have some husbands remember their wedding anniversary is to get married on his birthday. Also if you are looking for the best place to hide your husband's anniversary present then you should try the ironing basket. Certainly men are usually not too smart at remembering dates, but on anniversaries, if the husband is on the ball, he may have forgotten the past but certainly will not forget the present.

As long as he is not like the mean old Scot who insisted on his wedding taking place on 29 February; the reason being he would only have to buy flowers and chocolates every four years.

> IN THE EARLY DAYS OF MARRIAGE MEN AND WOMEN
> WANT EACH OTHER. IN LATER YEARS THEY
> NEED EACH OTHER.

It is pleasant to think back to those early days of romance. Hopefully everyone can remember them. No doubt lying in some dusty attic is a box tied with ribbon. Inside are all the sentimental billets-doux from those special early days. Wouldn't it be nice to read them all over again. Aaaah!

Remember when you phoned just to hear his voice. Remember him opening doors for you, pulling out your chair and even walking on the outside of the pavement. Remember your special times together, the songs, the flowers. The magic may change but the spell still works.

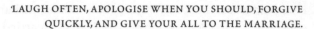

'LAUGH OFTEN, APOLOGISE WHEN YOU SHOULD, FORGIVE
QUICKLY, AND GIVE YOUR ALL TO THE MARRIAGE.

What about the love life? It has now been proved that there is a link between marriage, sex and astrology. If you've been married over twenty years sex happens once in a blue moon. One of the problems is that those dangerous curves may have become extended detours.

An old Scots couple were lying in bed and the wife said wistfully, 'Do you remember when we were first married and got into bed, you hardly gave me time to get my stockings off?'

'Aye,' sighed the old man. 'An' noo' you'd have time tae knit yersel' a pair.'

If you are married for a long time then it is quite an achievement. Some anniversaries, though, can be more meaningful than others. Ten years is a tin anniversary, which means she has been opening them for ten years. If you have been married for fifteen years that is crystal, which means that by this time your wife can see right through you. Married for thirty years is pearl, which means that after all these years you feel like stringing each other up. And if you make sixty years then you may understand this:

> Granpaw's whiskers, old and grey,
> Often got in Granny's way.
> Once she chewed them in her sleep
> Thinking they were shredded wheat.

Anniversaries

(The names come from the gifts traditionally deemed suitable for each year)

First	Cotton	Fifteenth	Crystal
Second	Paper	Twentieth	China
Third	Leather	Twenty-fifth	Silver
Fourth	Silk	Thirtieth	Pearl
Fifth	Wood	Thirty-fifth	Coral
Sixth	Iron	Fortieth	Ruby
Seventh	Wool	Forty-fifth	Sapphire
Eighth	Bronze	Fiftieth	Gold
Ninth	Pottery	Fifty-fifth	Emerald
Tenth	Tin	Sixtieth	Diamond
Twelfth	Linen	Seventieth	Platinum

It may be easy to make a few men fall in love with you over a few years, but to make one man love you for fifty years; *that* is a real achievement. Hopefully at this stage both faces will be a juxtaposition of not just wrinkles, but laughter lines, indicating that, for all its ups and downs, the marriage has, in the main, been fun. But at the end of the day no one can dissect a marriage except the two principals. Just contemplate the following:

> The word 'auld maid' would make ye scunner,
> But what's a husband, ye may wunner.
> He's the man to whom ye tell the care,
> Ye wouldnae hae were he no' there.
> But harsh my words, I call to mind,
> The bliss, the joy, the actions kind
> O' youthful love. Young married bliss.
> No human feeling sweeter is.
> And even in the autumn of your years
> A hand tae clasp, a smile that cheers.
> A real guid man's a precious prize,
> That nae sane wummin would despise.
>
> M. IRVING MBE

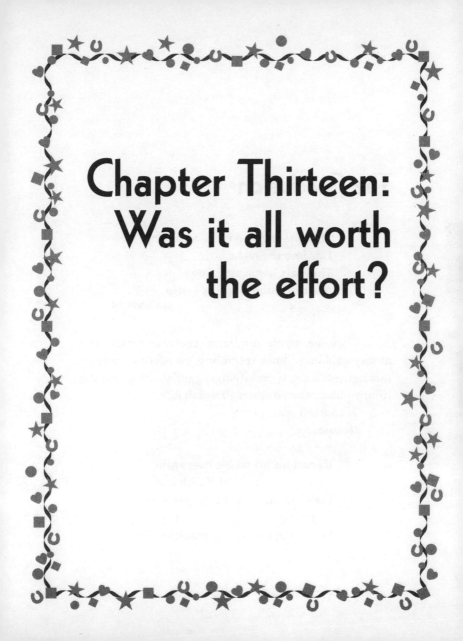

Chapter Thirteen:
Was it all worth
the effort?

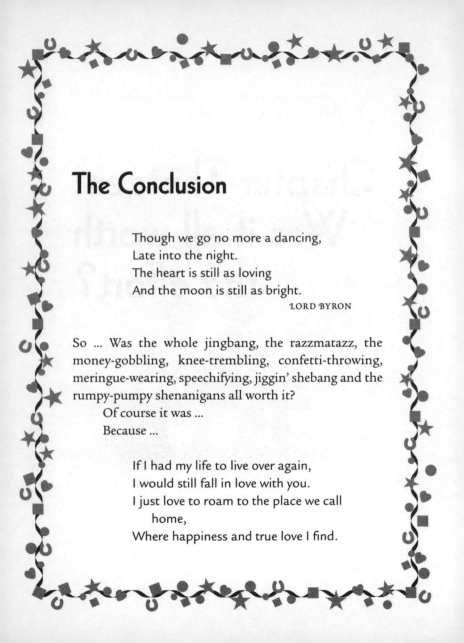

The Conclusion

Though we go no more a dancing,
Late into the night.
The heart is still as loving
And the moon is still as bright.

LORD BYRON

So ... Was the whole jingbang, the razzmatazz, the money-gobbling, knee-trembling, confetti-throwing, meringue-wearing, speechifying, jiggin' shebang and the rumpy-pumpy shenanigans all worth it?

Of course it was ...

Because ...

If I had my life to live over again,
I would still fall in love with you.
I just love to roam to the place we call
home,
Where happiness and true love I find.

I loved you when our vows were spoken,
Then we walked down the aisle hand in
    hand.
If I had my life to live over again,
I would still fall in love with you.

Glossary of Wedding Preparation Requirements...

...Including Many Optional Extras

Bar Is it an 'all-inclusive' wedding or a 'pay-bar'? May depend on your Lotto results.

Best man His selection is critical to the success of the event. Will he be capable of carrying out all his duties and holding his drink?

Booking the venue for the ceremony Get written confirmation of date, times and costs, or you may turn up only to find another wedding in progress.

Bridal flower jewellery Lily-of-the-valley, roses and calla lilies are fashionable.

Bridesmaids Will they be prettier than the bride? Have they practised their catching?

Bridesmaids' dresses Style, theme and colour of bridesmaids' dresses must not upstage the Star.

Bubble-blowing sets Guests sing 'I'm Forever Blowing Bubbles' as they have fun during the meal. Gets everyone in the party spirit.

Candelabras Handy if the lights fail.

Caricaturist Have your guests captured on the back of their menus. It's fun and a terrific souvenir to find in your loft thirty years on!

Ceilidh band, disco or whatever If it is a posh do, make sure you have musicians who are also well turned out. Ask them not to be too loud otherwise older guests will all sit fiddling with their hearing aids.

Champagne and canapés Makes it awfa posh, sure it does...

Champagne fountain Up-market idea, and you get to drink the contents!

Children's entertainer Will simply *make* the wedding for the weans.

Children's activity favour packs Include a colouring book, crayons and chocolates. Keeps the wee souls from running around daft.

Chocolate fountain The trouble with these is that once your guests have tasted the contents, you can't get them away from the fountain.

Choir Can add another dimension to the occasion as long as they sing in tune.

Church bells Ding dong the bells are gonna chime, but only if the ceremony is in a church and you give a few quid to the campanologists! Nice idea, though.

Confetti, rice, rose petals Obtain permission from venues as to whether they allow you to throw confetti. If not, ask guests to bring rice... it also feeds the birds!

Decorations for the ceremony Row-end posies. Useful for guests to pinch if they've forgotten their buttonhole.

Disposable cameras for tables Gives you some informal photos to supplement your wedding album.

Dress The costume for the star of the show is vital. A late fitting in the days before the wedding is advisable to deal with the various effects of panic-eating or dieting. Just remember to have 'Something old, something new, something borrowed, something blue'.

Evening reception arrangements Determine the number of evening guests; will there be enough seats and food for them all? Can they be kept entertained outside the reception room if the best man speaks for thirty-five minutes?

Favours Sugared almonds, a candle, Scottish tablet or even Edinburgh rock.

Fireworks Depends on the reception venue, weather and time of year. Great if it's all going like a damp squib!

First-night accommodation Perhaps a chauffeur-driven car to take you to the airport the following day, assuming you both have survived the night!

Flower girls Must be cute and toilet trained.

Flowers Buttonholes or sprigs of white heather. Great, as long as you don't have hay fever.

Gear for the groom Highland dress for the true Scotsman, or top hat and tails, or a lounge suit? Or even the full 'Bonnie Prince Charlie' rig-out for the weekend Jacobite warrior?

Gift list What do you need, want, aspire to ... and are your guests going to come up with the lolly?

Gift for all the guests Depends on your budget and whether *Hello!* magazine is 'sponsoring' your wedding.

Gifts For best man, ushers and bridesmaids. Souvenirs of their contribution to the great day.

Gifts for the parents Perhaps a wee ornament. After all, you've sponged off them for years, so you have.

Gratuities Can you trust your best man with the cash to disburse?

Guard of honour A canopy of drawn military swords for the bridal couple as they emerge from the ceremony looks great. Don't have people with shaky hands.

There's meant to be eight of us lads here from his plumbing firm, but the rest have all rung in to say they could be a little late –

Guest book Lets all the guests put in their comments (nice ones, hopefully) and their best wishes for the happy duo.

Guest-friendly reception location Hotel, club, pub, town hall, castle, even a house-party reception? Wheelchair access must also be considered. Will there be a 'red carpet' outside for the bridal party? Is the dance area large enough, and have the agreements all been confirmed in writing? Also, preferential room rates for guests and for the bridal suite?

Guest list The occasion on which you write out all the potential guest names, then realise it is far too many to accommodate and totally beyond your budget. You ask your intended, 'Who are they, anyway?' and get the reply, 'Second cousins of my mother twice removed.' Well, they're out for a start! And is there to be provision for children or is it adults only?

Hairdos and beauty treatment The 'best of the best' is required. Everyone is a celebrity for the day. An advance run through is fundamental, especially with a new hairdresser.

Helium-filled balloons For table numbers or with the happy pair's names on them.

Honeymoon Make it a wee bit special so you can look back on it with fond memories ... hopefully!

Ice sculptures A wonderful focal point for your guests' photos. A bust of the bride and groom is the ultimate. Also handy to cool your G&T.

Inoculation requirements Certain countries may require these before you fly to your honeymoon destination. The last thing you want is the dreaded lurgie.

Lighting of a wedding candle Not on top of the cake, and you don't blow it out! Often part of a church ceremony or at the top table.

Limo/vintage car/carriage and horse/helicopter/rickshaw Must be reliable and have champagne in the back. You may want to have 'good luck pennies' ready to throw to well-wishers.

Love-birds A cage in the foyer of the reception venue?

'Who said anything about Good Luck hugs?'

Lucky chimney sweep You'll be lucky to find one nowadays! It used to be considered lucky if the bride met a soot-covered chimney sweep on the way to the wedding. The sweep was considered to have magical powers associated with the hearth and lum, the centre of the family home.

Lucky horseshoes The old story goes that the devil asked a blacksmith to shoe his single hoof. When the blacksmith recognised his customer he carried out the task as painfully as possible, until the devil pleaded for mercy. The blacksmith released him on condition that in future he never entered an establishment where a horseshoe was displayed.

Marriage documentation This is fundamental, otherwise you will merely be inviting your guests to a party!

Master of ceremonies Keeps the event on schedule and everybody up to date on what's happening ... hopefully!

Memory candle In remembrance of those who would have liked to have been at the wedding but who are ill, have passed on, or just couldn't come for other reasons.

Menu and dietary requirements Another tricky bit of planning required here. Vegetarian? Gluten-free? Dairy-free? Kosher-meat? Or just 'Unbelievably Greedy'?

Names A decision has to be made as to whether the bride will take his name, retain her own name, or will they combine monikers?

New name on passport Or do you just fly off on honeymoon using the old one? If you are taking your husband's name, apply for a new passport two months before the wedding.

Newspaper announcements Make sure both families agree the wording otherwise you may have a problem!

Outfits for mothers of the bride and groom Some diplomatic consultation may reassure, and ensure, no clashing.

Page boys Cute, definitely toilet trained, and without a snotty nose.

Personalised table wine and whisky Great souvenirs of the occasion, especially if the contents are good.

Photos and video Select appropriate background music for video; not 'You've Lost That Lovin' Feeling'!

Piper You can't do better than the skirl o' the pipes!

Place cards Make sure you spell the names correctly. Some folks get indigestion over a missing 'a' in Mac.

Powerpoint slide show One of photos from the bride and groom's childhoods. Not the ones of you paddling naked on the beach at St Andrews.

Programme of events Times and details of the day's proceedings.

Rings Have initials and date engraved inside so you can remember who you married, and the anniversary date.

Show of presents Bit old-fashioned but still goes on. Excuse for some of the hen-night girls to practise swallying the hard stuff. Sometimes replaced by the American-style 'bridal shower'.

Singer/string quartet/harpist For during the signing of register or meal. Nice touch and keeps the troops from getting restless.

Sky lanterns Usually lucky Chinese ones that float off into the night sky and get the UFO brigade all excited. Get someone who knows what they are doing to light them.

Special bouquets For presentation to both mums during the groom's speech. Good for a wee greet.

Table decorations/flowers Not to be sniffed at. Try to fit in with the overall colour scheme of the day.

Table magician Keeps the guests' minds off the stringy chicken.

Table plan The biggest minefield since the D-Day beaches!

(a) Will the bride's mother and stepmother scratch each other's eyes out unless seated at opposite ends of the top table?

(b) Should the Edinburgh and Glasgow guests sit at 'mixed' tables?

(c) Would the little bridesmaids be better back with their mothers than getting ketchup all over the top table?

(d) Should the best man and chief bridesmaid be seated together, have seats adjacent to their respective partners, or do you just book them a room?

Toasting goblets Special glasses to be used by the bride and groom at the top table.

Visas Make sure they are going to let you into the honeymoon country of your choice.

Wedding cake A heated knife is recommended for the slicing of those sugary-pink rosebuds.

Wedding fans Ones you use to keep you cool (in the hot, steamy, balmy Scottish summertime!).

Wedding insurance Could cover a number of potential problems, like illness of the key parties. The policy is unlikely to address weather ... well, it is Scotland. Do make sure you arrange the insurance before you pay any deposits.

Wedding rehearsal Optional, but a good idea as it saves you ad-libbing on the big day.

Wedding stationery 'Save-the-Date' cards, formal invitations, map of how to get to venues, programme and menu cards. Perhaps have printed on your stationery a couple of sweet, old, family, sepia-style photos, lines from your favourite poem or song, or your favourite photo of you both together. Just don't forget to put the time and date on the invitation as some have done.

Wedding theme A unique theme such as colour or design for the special day.

White doves Watch in case they leave 'calling cards' as they fly off.

Witnesses People capable of putting more than just an 'X' on the register.